THE
EARTH
SCIENCE
BOOK

Crust 1. coffee can / crisco'd   4 or small 1 loaf   ? loaves
2. thaw lake
3. cut

4. crust
jelly
butterscotch candy
crunchy peanut butter to
mantle
outer core
jelly
butterscotch
inner core

Other Titles of Interest from Wiley

The Ocean Book, Center for Marine Conservation

Projects for a Healthy Planet, Shar Levine and Allison Grafton

Spectacular Science Project series:
Janice VanCleave's Animals
Janice VanCleave's Earthquakes
Janice VanCleave's Gravity
Janice VanCleave's Machines
Janice VanCleave's Magnets
Janice VanCleave's Molecules

Flying Start Science series:
Action
Flight
Light
Pattern
Structure
Water

David Suzuki's Looking At series:
Looking at the Body
Looking at the Environment
Looking at Insects
Looking at Plants
Looking at Senses
Looking at Weather

The Complete Handbook of Science Fair Projects, Julianne Bochinski

The Thomas Edison Book of Easy and Incredible Experiments,
The Thomas Alva Edison Foundation

Science for Every Kid series:
Janice VanCleave's Astronomy for Every Kid
Janice VanCleave's Biology for Every Kid
Janice VanCleave's Chemistry for Every Kid
Janice VanCleave's Earth Science for Every Kid
Janice VanCleave's Math for Every Kid
Janice VanCleave's Physics for Every Kid

THE EARTH SCIENCE BOOK

ACTIVITIES FOR KIDS

Dinah Zike

Illustrations by Jessie J. Flores

John Wiley & Sons, Inc.
New York · Chichester · Brisbane · Toronto · Singapore

Design and Production: Dinah-Might Activities, Inc.
Art Director: Ignacio Salas-Humara
Illustrator: Jessie J. Flores
Photography: © 1993 Ignacio Salas-Humara
Special Thanks to Kate Bradford, Jan Dorough, Mae and
Lyle Fjelsted, Kim Hendrickson, Suzie Kempf,
Kari Morrison, and Suzanne Powers

The publisher and the author have made every reasonable effort to ensure that the experiments and activities in this book are safe when conducted as instructed but assume no responsability for any damage caused or sustained while performing the experiments or activities in this book. Parents, guardians, and/or teachers should supervise young readers who undertake the experiments and activities in this book.

In recognition of the importance of preserving what has been written, it is a policy of John Wiley & Sons, Inc., to have books of enduring value published in the United States printed on acid-free paper, and we exert our best efforts to that end.

Printed in the United States of America

10 9 8 7 6 5 4 3 2 1

Contents

THE
EARTH
SCIENCE
BOOK

Chapter 1

The Earth

You can see trillions of miles above the Earth when you look up at the night sky. If it is a clear night, sit with your family or friends in a location where you can relax and watch the stars. The light you see from the tiny specks has traveled for thousands of years on an unimaginable journey through six billion miles or more of darkness before reaching your eyes and the planet Earth.

Earth seems so large when we are looking down at its surface from an airplane or when we look out of the window of a moving car, but it seems so small when we look up into the vastness of the night sky. Earth is small when compared to the universe. In this chapter we will look at Earth as a minute speck in the universe, a small planet in a solar system, and a large sphere of rock and minerals.

Earth's Place in the Universe

It is impossible to imagine how huge and endless space is and how small the Earth is within this space. If we compared the groups of stars that make up space to drops of rain in a thunderstorm, the Earth would be only a tiny part of one of the raindrops. Close your eyes and try to imagine Earth as a dot within infinite space.

The Universe

This infinite space is the **universe**. It is made up of countless stars that form star groups, or **galaxies**. Each galaxy contains hundreds of millions of stars, planets, asteroids, moons, and dust. Scientists have counted over 10 billion galaxies. Think how many star groups there must be that cannot be seen or counted, even with the strongest telescope.

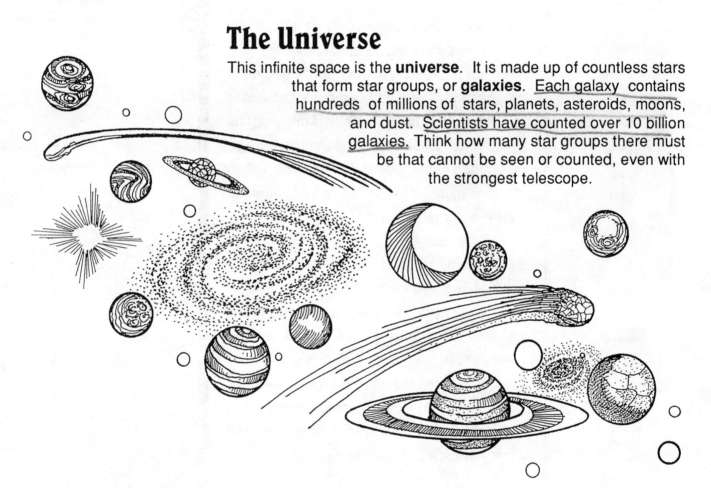

The Milky Way

Earth is located in a galaxy called the **Milky Way**. Like a big propeller, the Milky Way galaxy is flat and spiral-shaped, and it turns slowly in space. It contains about 100 billion stars. Our Sun is one of these stars. Most of the stars are clustered in the center of the galaxy, and the rest, including our Sun, form the three "arms" of the Milky Way's propeller shape.

You are here!

The Solar System

Our Sun is surrounded by nine planets and their moons. Each planet moves along an **elliptical**, or oval-shaped, path around the Sun. This group — the Sun, the planets, and their moons — is called the **Solar System**.

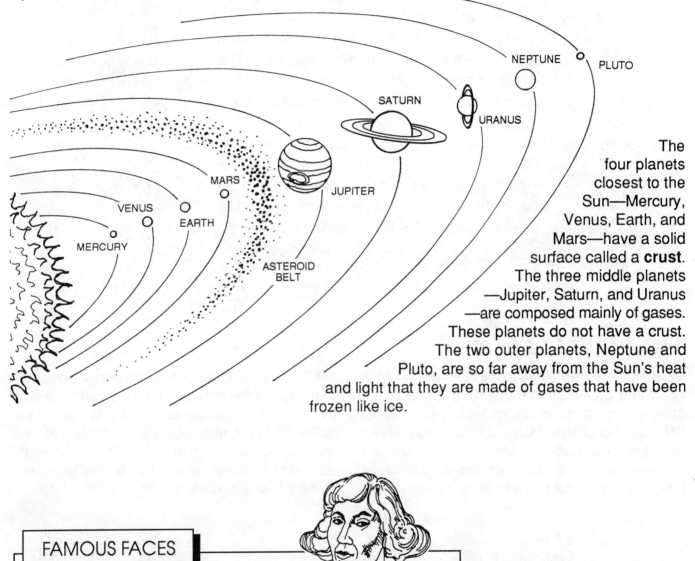

The four planets closest to the Sun—Mercury, Venus, Earth, and Mars—have a solid surface called a **crust**. The three middle planets —Jupiter, Saturn, and Uranus —are composed mainly of gases. These planets do not have a crust. The two outer planets, Neptune and Pluto, are so far away from the Sun's heat and light that they are made of gases that have been frozen like ice.

FAMOUS FACES

NICOLAUS COPERNICUS
(Polish astronomer, 1473-1543)

Before and during Copernicus' lifetime, scientists thought the Sun and the planets circled around the Earth. In 1543, Copernicus theorized that the Sun was the center of the Solar System. Although many scientists disagreed with him and he could not prove his theory, he challenged people to think about his new idea. A hundred years passed before Copernicus was proven to be right. After the invention of the telescope, the observations of Galileo proved that the Earth moves around the Sun.

A Star Is Born

Five billion years ago, the Sun and its planets did not exist. Instead, there was a huge, spinning cloud of hot gases and tiny, dustlike particles. The very fast turning motion of this cloud caused the heaviest particles to be pulled toward the cloud's center at high speeds. The speeding particles crashed into each other with great force, producing heat and pressure. The particles began to burn. A huge ball of swirling, exploding, fiery-hot particles collected at the center of the spinning cloud, giving off light and heat energy. Our **Sun** was formed.

The Planets Form

Many particles remained in the outer areas of the cloud and circled around the newly formed Sun. These distant particles and gases began to collect into clouds of different sizes at different distances from the Sun. Each spinning cloud pulled the particles within it together into a sphere, or ball shape, and the **planets** were formed.

The clouds closest to the Sun were made of the denser, heavier particles pulled toward the Sun by its gravity. (See pages 16-17.) These clouds formed solid, heavy planets. Lighter particles and gases were left to form the clouds most distant from the Sun, and these clouds formed planets that are made of gases.

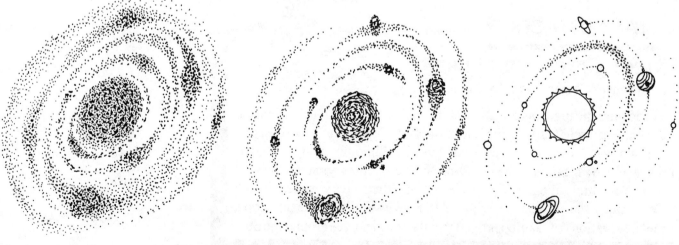

ACTION ACTIVITY
THE SOLAR SYSTEM

You can make a model of the Solar System to scale. This means that your mini-Solar System would show the relative size of the planets compared to each other and the Sun, and their relative distances from each other and the Sun. Make your Sun 27 inches (68.6 cm) in diameter and allow 1 inch (2.5 cm) to equal 20 million miles (32 million km). Here are the dimensions and distances you need to make your model.

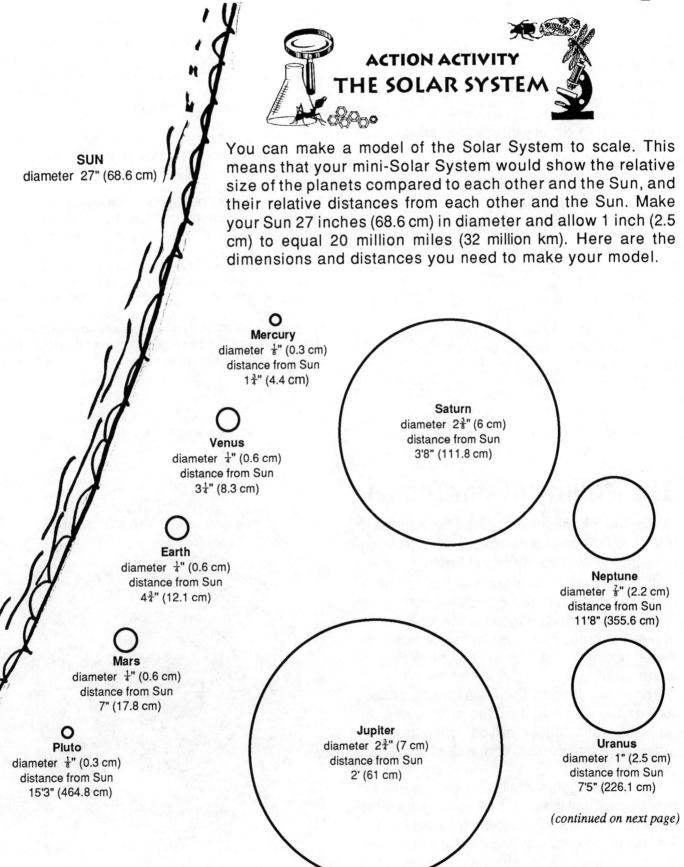

SUN
diameter 27" (68.6 cm)

Mercury
diameter $\frac{1}{8}$" (0.3 cm)
distance from Sun
1$\frac{3}{4}$" (4.4 cm)

Venus
diameter $\frac{1}{4}$" (0.6 cm)
distance from Sun
3$\frac{1}{4}$" (8.3 cm)

Earth
diameter $\frac{1}{4}$" (0.6 cm)
distance from Sun
4$\frac{3}{4}$" (12.1 cm)

Mars
diameter $\frac{1}{4}$" (0.6 cm)
distance from Sun
7" (17.8 cm)

Pluto
diameter $\frac{1}{8}$" (0.3 cm)
distance from Sun
15'3" (464.8 cm)

Saturn
diameter 2$\frac{3}{8}$" (6 cm)
distance from Sun
3'8" (111.8 cm)

Neptune
diameter $\frac{7}{8}$" (2.2 cm)
distance from Sun
11'8" (355.6 cm)

Jupiter
diameter 2$\frac{3}{4}$" (7 cm)
distance from Sun
2' (61 cm)

Uranus
diameter 1" (2.5 cm)
distance from Sun
7'5" (226.1 cm)

(continued on next page)

(continued from previous page)

MATERIALS
- **large sheet of poster paper**
- **1 brass brad**
- **ruler or tape measure**
- **8 inches (17.1 cm) of yarn or strong string**
- **pencil**
- **self-hardening clay**

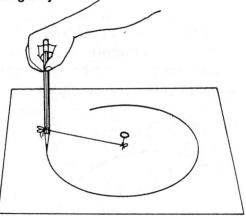

1. Place the poster paper on the floor or a large table. Push the brass brad through the center of the poster paper, and tie one end of the string around the brad. Tie the other end of the string around the pencil. The remaining string should be about 6¾ inches (17.1 cm) long.

2. Stand the pencil upright and draw a circle as illustrated. This circle should have a diameter of about 27 inches (68.6 cm). Cut out the circle of poster paper and label it "SUN."

3. Form the planets with the clay. Make the diameter as close as you can to the measurements given. Compare the sizes of your clay "planets" with the illustrations on page 5.

4. Find an open area, such as a park, and place the Sun 93 inches (7'9"; 236.2 cm) from the Earth. Use the chart to help you place the other planets the correct distances away from the Sun. Look at your model. Remember, one inch equals 20 million miles. Now you can see how the Sun and planets compare in size and how far apart they are. The Sun is 93 million miles away from the Earth. How far is it from Pluto?

The Making of Our Planet

During the formation of the Solar System, one of the clouds of particles and gases circling close to the Sun formed into the planet **Earth.**

As the heaviest particles were pulled to the center of this cloud, the Earth's hot core of iron and nickel formed. Lighter particles collected above the core, and even lighter particles collected above this to form the outer layers of the Earth's crust.

The newly formed Earth was made of liquid rock and liquid metal. It had no solid surface and no liquid water. It took millions of years for the outer surface of Earth to cool enough to become solid.

Gases, the lightest of all particles, floated close to the surface of the solid ball, forming the **atmosphere**. This first air was very different from the air we breathe today because it was mostly hydrogen and helium with little or no oxygen.

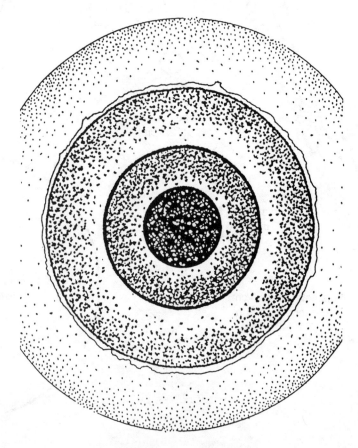

The Planet Earth — One of a Kind

Even after the Earth formed a solid crust, volcanoes continued to spew molten rock from beneath the Earth's surface. The volcanoes also released gases and water vapor, which formed clouds. These clouds released the first rains, which helped cool the Earth as they collected on Earth's surface, creating the oceans.

Constant Changes

The Earth continued to cool, allowing gases that were trapped in the crust to be released. Carbon dioxide, nitrogen, and oxygen gases formed a new atmosphere. Over millions of years, the temperature of Earth became lower and more constant. Gradually this new atmosphere protected the Earth more and more from the Sun's harmful rays, and somewhere in the shallows of the ancient oceans the first life forms — microscopic plants — developed.

Scientists believe the Earth formed $4\frac{1}{2}$ billion years ago. To get an idea of how much $4\frac{1}{2}$ billion really is, think about this. If you took a ream of $8\frac{1}{2}$" x 11" paper (500 sheets per ream) and cut the paper into 1-inch squares (500 sheets thick), a ream would produce 88 stacks or a total of 44,000 paper squares. To get 1 billion paper squares, you would need 22,728 reams of paper. For $4\frac{1}{2}$ billion squares, you would need 102,276 reams (51,138,000 sheets)!

Remember the fairy tale "Goldilocks and the Three Bears"? Goldilocks was looking for a perfect environment with good food and a comfortable shelter. She wanted everything to be just right — not too hot and not too cold, not too big and not too small, not too hard and not too soft.

Perfect for Life

Earth is different from the other planets that formed around the Sun. It is the only planet in the Solar System that provides just the right environment for life to exist.

Earth is neither too hot nor too cold; it is just the right distance from the Sun to get the right amount of heat for a wide range of animal and plant species to live. Earth is just the right size — not so small that its gravity would be too weak to hold the atmosphere, and not so large that its gravity would hold too much atmosphere, including harmful gases. Earth is neither too hard nor too soft. It is a solid planet with 70.8% of its solid surface covered by a liquid: water. Compare Earth with Jupiter, a planet made entirely of gases, or Neptune, a planet totally covered in ice.

The Earth is a special planet within our Solar System because it is the only planet with liquid water; its orbit is the perfect distance from the Sun for receiving just the right amount of light and heat energy; it has the only atmosphere that contains the exact mixture of gases (oxygen and nitrogen) necessary for life to exist; and it has water vapor clouds and a special layer of atmosphere, the ozone layer, above the clouds to act as a shield from the Sun's harmful radiation.

ACTION ACTIVITY
JUST RIGHT
FOR LIFE

We can't visit Mercury and Pluto to do this activity, but we can simulate the conditions on these planets to find out why the life forms we find on Earth can't exist there.

MATERIALS
- dried beans
- 3 small paper cups (4-6 oz.)
- soil
- aluminum foil (12" or 30.5 cm long)
- medium-sized shoe box
- 3 thermometers

1. Plant 3 bean seeds in 3 small cups of soil. Water the soil to keep it damp, and wait until the beans sprout.

2. Label the cups "Mercury," "Earth," and "Pluto."

3. Insert a thermometer ¾" (2 cm) into each of the three cups of soil.

4. When the bean sprouts are about 2" (5 cm) tall, place the "Mercury" cup in an open box lined with aluminum foil and place the box outside in direct sunlight. Do not water. Mercury has no water, and is extremely hot.

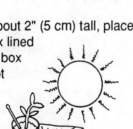

5. Place the "Earth" cup near a window, in the shade. Water once every 2 or 3 days. This approximates the conditions on Earth: rain, some sun, and shade provided by clouds.

6. Place the "Pluto" cup in the freezer. Do not water. Pluto is so far from the Sun that it gets very little sunlight, and any water on the planet would be frozen.

7. Take temperature readings at noon and at 6 P.M. for each cup. Find the highest and lowest temperatures for each "planet."

- What happens to each plant after a week?
- What temperature do you think is "just right" for plant life?
- Why else is Earth "just right" for plant life?
- What would happen if you planted a seedling on Mercury or Pluto?

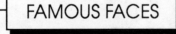

FAMOUS FACES

BENJAMIN BANNEKER
(American astronomer and mathematician, 1731-1806)

From 1792 to 1806 Benjamin Banneker published an almanac for which he did all the astronomical calculations and made all the weather predictions. Even Thomas Jefferson, the third President of the United States, praised Banneker's work. His accomplishments were especially amazing because he had very little formal schooling. As a child he had few books, so for fun he would create difficult problems for himself to solve. His almanac was a continuation of his love of problem-solving.

Earth's Seasons

Earth is just right for life, but conditions on Earth are not always the same. If you could place a video camera in your yard or in a park near your house, and allow it to record for a year, you would see how much the Earth changes around you during that time. The conditions change because Earth is constantly changing its position in space.

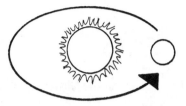

One revolution equals 365 days.

Revolution

All of the planets of the Solar System revolve around the Sun. It takes the Earth 365 days, 6 hours, 9 minutes, and 10 seconds to make one orbit, or **revolution,** around the Sun. This is why we use 365 days to measure one year of time. Every fourth year is **leap year**; it has 366 days to make up for the extra hours that accumulated during the four previous years. The Earth tilts a little as it circles the Sun. This imaginary tilt line running through the center of the Earth from the North Pole to the South Pole is called the **axis**. The Earth is tilted at an angle of 23.5 degrees. This angle of tilt is important, because it is responsible for the **seasons.**

ACTION ACTIVITY
SEASONS

The seasons of the year are different, depending on whether you live in the Northern or Southern Hemisphere — even though it is the same day and month in both places.

MATERIALS

• a flashlight or lamp without its shade
• a globe

1. Place the globe on a table with the top of the axis pointing toward you. In a darkened room, aim the beam of the flashlight at 23.5 degrees north latitude, the Tropic of Cancer. This represents summer in the Northern Hemisphere and winter in the Southern Hemisphere. The hours of daylight are longer in the Northern Hemisphere. Can you determine why?

2. Position the globe so that the top of the axis is pointing away from you. Aim the beam of the flashlight at 23.5 degrees south latitude, the Tropic of Capricorn. Now it is summer in the Southern Hemisphere and winter in the Northern Hemisphere.

The Changing Seasons

The **seasons** are the result of two things — the Earth's revolution around the Sun and the tilt of its axis. During its 365-day revolution, the Earth faces the Sun at different angles, so its surface receives direct sunlight on different areas of its surface at different times.

For about half of the period of the Earth's revolution around the Sun, the top half, or **Northern Hemisphere**, of the Earth leans toward the Sun. At this angle the Northern Hemisphere gets the most direct sunlight, and the Southern Hemisphere gets the least; so in the Northern Hemi-sphere it is **summer**, and in the Southern Hemisphere it is **winter**.

At the opposite side of the revolution, the Earth's axis tilts away from the Sun. The Northern Hemisphere gets the least direct sunlight, while the Southern Hemisphere gets the most. It is winter in the Northern Hemisphere and summer in the Southern Hemisphere.

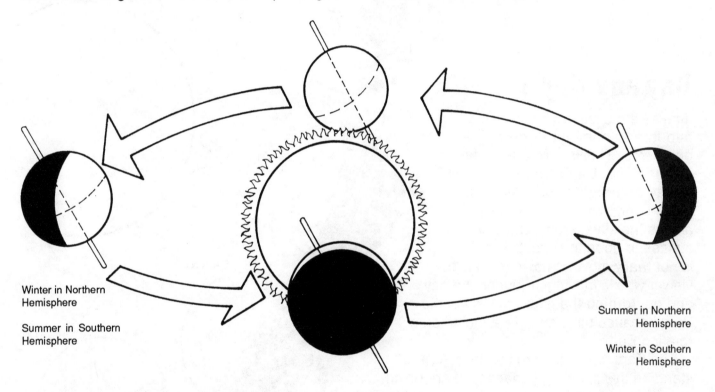

Winter in Northern Hemisphere

Summer in Southern Hemisphere

Summer in Northern Hemisphere

Winter in Southern Hemisphere

During the **fall** and **spring** seasons, the Earth's axis is almost parallel to the Sun's. This is a time when the Northern and Southern hemispheres receive nearly the same amount of sunlight.

The **Equator** (the imaginary line dividing the Earth into Northern and Southern Hemispheres) is exposed to direct sunlight during the entire 365-day revolution. That is why there are no drastic seasonal temperature changes in areas around the Equator; it is summer all year. Conditions are very different at the Earth's poles, which never receive direct sunlight and always experience winter.

Each year there are two days when the hours of daylight and darkness are the same length: on March 20 or 21 and September 22 or 23. These days are called the **vernal** and **autumnal equinoxes,** and they mark the beginning of spring and fall.

 EARTH'S ROTATION

Earth's Rotation

The Earth **rotates**, or spins on its axis, much faster than it revolves around, or orbits, the Sun. That is why a day is so much shorter than a year on Earth.

Day and Night

It takes the Earth 23 hours and 56 minutes to complete one rotation on its axis. This is how a day of time is measured. Earth's rotation results in day and night, and a viewer on Earth seems to see the Sun move across the sky during a day from sunrise to noon to sunset. The Sun is not really moving, however. It is the viewer who is moving in (during the day) and out (during the night) of view of the Sun, because the viewer is standing on a rotating Earth.

The Earth spins toward the east. As you stand on this spinning surface, you are being moved eastward. That is why the Sun "comes up" in the east and the Moon "rises" in the east. The Sun and Moon are first seen to the east as the Earth brings you around to their positions in space, and they disappear in the west as the Earth continues to turn.

If the Earth did not rotate, one half of its surface would get baked and overheated in constant sunlight, and the other half of its surface would freeze in total darkness. As the Earth rotates, the heated half moves away from the Sun and cools off, and the cooled half comes around and is warmed.

MORNING

NOON

EVENING

NIGHT

12

Earth's Satellite

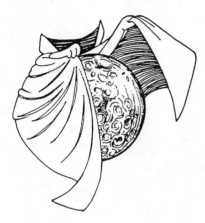

The Moon is hiding something from us: its dark side. Like the Earth, the Moon rotates and revolves, but unlike the Earth, the Moon takes the same amount of time to do both! The Moon revolves around the Earth, taking 29 days, 12 hours, and 44 minutes for each orbit. It takes the same amount of time to rotate, or spin, once. This means that as it orbits the Earth, the same side of the Moon is always facing us. It is impossible to see the Moon's "dark" side from Earth.

Held in Space

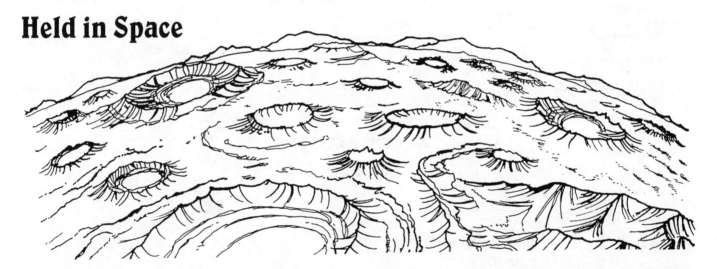

The Moon is 239,000 miles (384,000 km) away from the Earth. It is held in orbit around the Earth by the Earth's gravity. The Moon is just over $\frac{1}{4}$ the size of the Earth. Because of its small size, the Moon's gravity is very weak: only $\frac{1}{6}$ as strong as Earth's. (See pages 16-17.)

The Moon's gravitational pull is too weak to hold on to an atmosphere. Any gases it might have had early in its development drifted into space soon after it formed. The Earth's atmosphere protects it from meteors and other space objects because the friction of the air causes the objects to burn up before they strike the surface. (We can actually see this happen at night — we call it a "shooting star.") The Moon does not have an atmosphere to protect it, and meteors and other space objects have struck the Moon's surface for millions of years, creating the **craters**, or holes, we see today.

Without an atmosphere, the Moon also has no weather to erode its surface. There is no wind to change the shape of the craters and mountains. There is no water to form rain, no rivers to move soil and rocks. The first human footprint will remain outlined in the dust of the Moon's surface for the next million years!

Without an atmosphere or clouds to protect the Moon's surface from the Sun's rays, temperatures are extreme: hot enough (230° F, 110° C) to boil water during the day, and cold enough at night (-284°F, -140°C) to freeze almost anything.

Moon Timeline

4,600 MILLION YEARS AGO
The Moon is formed, along with the Earth and the rest of the Solar System. Continuous bombardment by thousands of small meteorites from space causes the surface to be pitted with craters.

4,200 MILLION YEARS AGO
Gigantic meteorites hit the Moon. The Sea of Tranquility, where American astronauts first landed, is an example of a giant meteorite crater.

4,000 MILLION YEARS AGO
Meteorite bombardment nearly stops. The rock beneath the crust begins to melt. Flows of lava break through the surface and flood the low crater floors, including the Sea of Tranquility and the other "seas."

3,900-3,500 MILLION YEARS AGO
The lava flows have become less frequent. The interior of the Moon begins to cool.

1,000 MILLION YEARS AGO
All volcanic activity ceases. The Moon becomes geologically "dead." For the next 1,000 million years the face of the Moon remains unchanged except for a few impacts from meteors. The most visible of these are the craters Tycho (formed 100 million years ago) and Copernicus (formed 900 million years ago).

JULY, 1969
Neil Armstrong, American astronaut with *Apollo 11*, lands and is the first human to set foot on the Moon.

ACTION ACTIVITY REFLECTED LIGHT

In this activity you will see how sunlight is reflected off the Moon onto the Earth.

MATERIALS
- golf ball
- flashlight
- a dark room

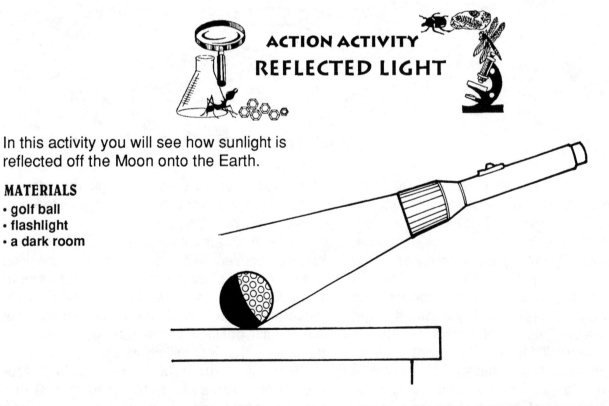

1. Place the golf ball on a table in the middle of the room.

2. Turn off the lights. Make the room as dark as possible. Can you see the golf ball? If the room is totally dark, you will not be able to see the ball.

3. Shine the flashlight on the golf ball. The golf ball can be seen because it reflects the light from the flashlight back to your eyes. This is what the Moon does; it reflects the light of the Sun back into space, and some of the light reaches Earth. It would be impossible to see the Moon in the darkness of space without reflected sunlight.

ACTION ACTIVITY
PHASES OF THE MOON

The Moon appears to be a slightly different shape each night. These shapes are called **phases** of the Moon.

MATERIALS
• a lamp without its shade
• a Styrofoam ball
• a pencil
• a dark room

1. Stick the pencil into the Styrofoam ball and use it as a handle for holding the ball.

2. Darken the room and turn on the lamp. The lamplight represents the Sun, the ball represents the Moon, and you represent the Earth.

3. Hold the ball between your body and the lamp, just above your head. The ball will appear dark. This is what happens when there is a new Moon. The Moon appears dark because it is between Earth and the Sun. It is not reflecting light toward Earth.

4. Walk the "Moon" around the lamp in a counterclockwise direction. Notice how the lighted part of the ball seems to change shape, from a thin line, or crescent, to a full moon, and then it begins to get smaller and smaller until you have no reflected light. This is what happens during the 29 days, 13 hours it takes the Moon to move around the Earth.

One half of the Moon is always lighted by the Sun; most of the time, however, only a part of the lighted half can be seen from Earth. This is because of our viewing angle on Earth. When you describe phases of the moon, the term **wax** means to increase in size and the term **wane** means to decrease in size. The moon waxes (increases) from new moon to full moon and then gradually wanes (decreases).

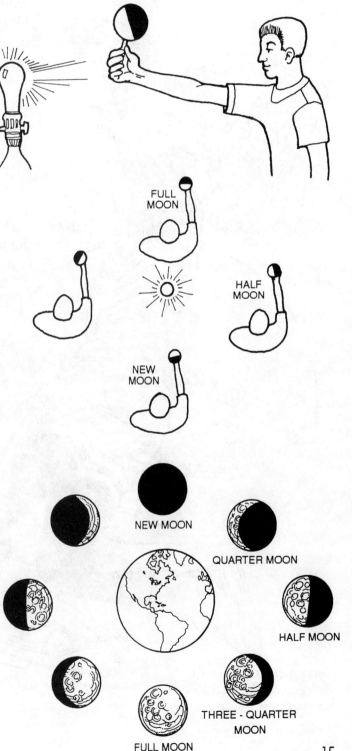

Gravity

Is it harder for you to walk up a steep hill than to walk down it? When you jump rope, is it easier to jump up or to land? Which is harder — to pull up in a chin-up or to lower yourself?

Everyone on Earth experiences the same effects, which all result from the same thing — **gravity**. Gravity makes rain fall and basketballs drop through hoops. It helps airplanes to land, keeps the Moon in its orbit, and makes push-ups difficult to do.

The Force Is with You

Gravity is an important force that affects everything on Earth. It is the force that five billion years ago caused the Earth to form out of a cloud of gas and particles. Gravity pulled all the parts of the cloud into the center, to form the solid sphere we live on — Earth. (See page 6.) We can't see gravity, but we can feel it. Gravity has been compared to a glue that keeps all things on Earth from floating into space. Earth's gravity tugs at everything on its surface and pulls at everything in the sky, including birds, planes, and clouds. Gravity even pulls at the Earth's air to keep it near the surface, where it is needed by plants and animals.

Gravity doesn't stop there. It pulls at objects in space, too. Gravity helps the Moon maintain its orbit around the Earth. The Earth's gravity tends to pull the Moon to the center of the Earth, but the Moon is moving too fast in space to fall. This delicate balancing act between the Earth's gravity and the Moon's revolution keeps the Moon from crashing into Earth or spinning off into space.

Some sports stars seem to defy gravity, but what goes up must come down!

The Changing Strength of Gravity

We feel the strength of gravity because we are on the surface of a very large object, the Earth. If we were to travel away from Earth's surface into space, the force of gravity on our bodies would be lessened, and we would become "weightless." Think about other circumstances that would change the pull of gravity on our bodies. What if you suddenly gained 50 pounds (22.5 kg)? The force of gravity between you and the Earth would be stronger, and you would have a harder time moving around.

When we think of the weight of an object, whether a feather or a truck, we can think of it as the measurement of the pull of the Earth's gravity on the object.

FAMOUS FACES

SIR ISAAC NEWTON
(English scientist, 1642-1727)

Newton was the first person to explain the effect of the force of gravity throughout the universe. He discovered that this force makes every object in the universe attract every other object. He also discovered that the strength of the force of gravity between objects is affected by two things: the **mass**, or amount of matter, of the objects and the distance between the objects. Large objects exert a stronger pull of gravity than smaller objects. Objects that are close together have a stronger pull of gravity than objects that are far apart.

Galileo, an Italian astronomer who lived from 1564 to 1642, showed the world that objects of different weights, when dropped from the same height, hit the ground at exactly the same time. He demonstrated that gravity pulls equally on all objects.

According to legend, Galileo went to the top of the Leaning Tower of Pisa in Italy and dropped a 10-pound and a 1-pound weight at the same time, while a group of curious townspeople watched. People were shocked when both weights hit the ground at the same time!

ACTION ACTIVITY
A FAST FALL

No one knows if the story about Galileo is true, but you can try the same thing with your friends. They might think that a heavy object would fall faster than a lighter object when dropped from the same height. See what happens!

MATERIALS
- **small rock**
- **piece of paper**

1. Take a piece of paper and crumple it up very, very tightly into a ball.

2. Find a rock about the same size as the paper ball.

3. Hold the rock and the paper ball in each hand, at the same height. Let go of both at the same time. Was Galileo right? Try it with other objects, such as a marble and a baseball. You might want to weigh the objects you are going to drop to see how weight affects how fast the objects fall.

Chapter 2

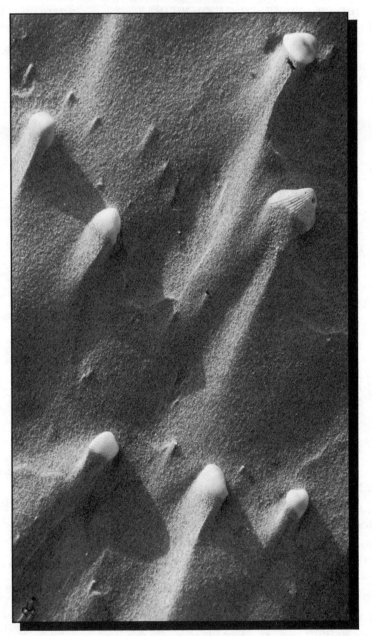

Matter

Pretend that you can place the planet Earth, including all of the people, plants, and animals that have ever lived on the Earth, on one side of a giant balance scale. Place the Earth as it is today, including all of the people, plants, and animals that are on Earth now, on the other side of the balance scale. Which would be heavier? They would weigh the same.

The Earth has had billions and billions of creatures living on it during its history, and yet the Earth does not get bigger. The Earth has had huge rocks and mountains that formed and then disappeared during its history, and still the Earth does not get bigger. What happened to all of the things that were once on the Earth?

The materials that compose everything on the Earth, and even the Earth itself, are constantly changing and being used over and over again. We will look at these materials, the "building blocks" of Earth and everything in it, in this chapter. We will investigate matter.

What Is Matter?

Name anything in the world that can be held, seen, or moved. What you have named is **matter.** Your body is matter; so is a book, a butterfly, a glass of juice, an airplane, and even the air through which the airplane flies. So what is matter?

Everything on Earth is matter. It is what all objects on Earth are made of. Anything that takes up space and has weight or mass is matter.

Three Kinds of Matter

Matter is usually divided into three groups — **solids, liquids,** and **gases.** When you hear someone talk about "the three states of matter," they are talking about these three groups. You can picture them like this:

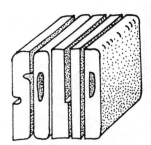

Solids have a definite shape.

Liquids take the shape of the container in which they are held.

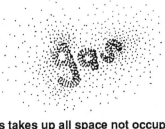

Gas takes up all space not occupied by a solid or a liquid. Gas has no shape of its own. It fills and takes up empty space.

We can compare the three parts of the Earth's surface with the three states of matter. The Earth has a solid surface, called a crust, or **lithosphere.** The Earth's ocean surface, or **hydrosphere**, is liquid. Above the crust and the ocean, there are gases, which form Earth's **atmosphere**.

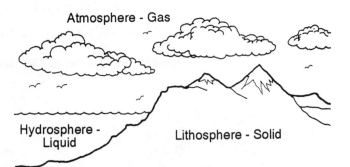

Atmosphere - Gas

Hydrosphere - Liquid

Lithosphere - Solid

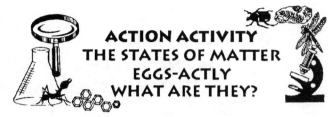

ACTION ACTIVITY
THE STATES OF MATTER
EGGS-ACTLY
WHAT ARE THEY?

Eggs can be dyed, boiled, scrambled, poached, and fried. We can also use an egg to illustrate the three basic states of matter.

MATERIALS

• **1 egg**
• **a small bowl or cup**
• **a plate**

1. Solid

Gently hold a fresh egg in your hand. It is a solid. The shape of the egg does not change easily. If you place the egg in the bowl, the egg will keep its shape.

Solid matter keeps its basic shape. Remove the egg from the bowl and place it on a plate. Does the egg retain its egg shape?

2. Liquid

Carefully tap the shell against the rim of the bowl to crack open the egg. Slowly spill the egg yolk and white into the bowl. Keep the eggshell. The inside of an egg is liquid.

A **liquid** takes the shape of its container. Before, the yolk and white had taken the shape of the eggshell; now they are the shape of the bowl. What would happen if you poured the yolk and white into a small square container?

3. Gas

Look inside the pieces of broken eggshell. In one end of the shell you will find a large bubble, or air pocket. Inside this space is gas, the third state of matter.

Gas is all around us; the air we breathe is a gas.

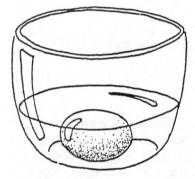

An egg is the perfect beginning for life. The solid shell is a strong, protective habitat. It is filled with nutritious liquid food and water. There is gas available for the baby chick to "breathe." The three states of matter that come together to form a chicken egg also come together to form life.

ACTION ACTIVITY
CHANGING THE
STATE OF MATTER

Matter can change from one state to another. With this activity you can change the same matter into all three states: liquid, solid, and gas.

MATERIALS

- freezer
- measuring cup
- fan
- 8 ounces (250 ml) water
- cake pan

1. Pour 8 ounces (250 ml) of water into the measuring cup.

2. Place the cup of water in the freezer. Allow it to freeze solid.

3. Remove the cup from the freezer. Has the liquid expanded? Is it above the 8-ounce (250-ml) mark on the measuring cup? Most matter contracts as it freezes. Water is unusual — it expands.

4. Remove the ice from the cup. Dip the cup in warm water for one minute if the ice is difficult to remove. Place the ice in the pan.

5. Find a warm place and turn a fan on so that it blows on the ice. How long does it take the ice to melt?

6. Pour the melted ice water back into the measuring cup. Measure the water. Is there 8 ounces (250 ml)? Was any water lost because of evaporation? If it was, the lost liquid has turned to gas — water vapor.

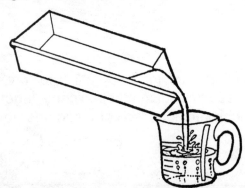

Element-ary Building Blocks

For hundreds of years scientists tried to solve the mystery of **matter.** What is matter made of? In the early 1800s, this mystery was solved. **John Dalton**, an English chemist and physicist, proposed that all matter is made of small particles called **atoms**. The ancient Greeks came up with the concept of the atom as the smallest particle of matter, but they did not know what an atom looked like or how it worked. Dalton's theory, called the **atomic theory**, explains the shape and structure and behavior of atoms. It says that atoms are the smallest complete (or whole) part of matter. They are the building blocks that make up all matter.

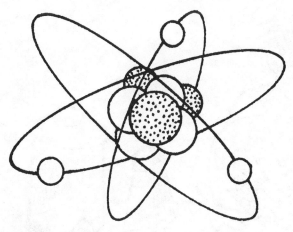

Atoms

The trouble with atoms is that they are so small they can't be seen, even with the most powerful microscope. The drawing on the left shows how we picture an atom. Atoms are made of three main **subatomic** (or smaller) parts — **protons**, **neutrons**, and **electrons**. The protons and neutrons form the center of the atom, called the **nucleus**. The electrons orbit around the nucleus.

There are **109** known types of atoms at this time. Each type of atom has a different combination of protons and neutrons in its nucleus and a different number of electrons orbiting the nucleus.

Molecules

To construct matter, one atom combines with another atom to form a larger building block called a **molecule.** Molecules can have anywhere from two to thousands of atoms. Most molecules are made from a combination of different types of atoms. These kinds of molecules are called **compounds.**

If we compare atoms to the letters of the alphabet, then molecules can be compared to words, because molecules are made of different combinations of atoms, just as words are spelled with different combinations of letters.

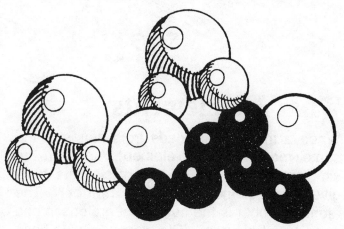

W o r d W a t c h

The word **atom** is from the Greek word **atomos,** which means **not able to be divided.**

Basic Elements

Even the best chef in the world could not cook all the recipes in the world with only 109 different ingredients. Yet everything on the Earth, living and nonliving, is made of only 109 ingredients called **elements**, in different recipes, or combinations. If we are going to fully understand how our Earth works, we need to understand the elements that compose everything on the Earth.

What Are Elements?

When a molecule is made from atoms of the same type, it is called an **element.** Atoms are the simplest form of an element. Scientists have given each element an **atomic number.** The atomic number is the number of protons in one atom of the element. The elements have been grouped according to their atomic numbers into a list called the **periodic table.** (See page 25.)

Everything on Earth is made of either molecules of pure elements or molecules made of combinations of elements (compounds).

Common Elements

If you walk along a beach or hike up a rocky hill, you are walking on the matter that forms the Earth's crust. Six elements comprise 94% of the Earth's crust. They are **oxygen, silicon, aluminum, iron, calcium,** and **sodium.**

Although it might not seem possible, the element oxygen, a gas, makes up nearly half the weight of the Earth's crust. This does not mean that the crust is full of oxygen bubbles. Oxygen is an element that combines very easily with other elements found in the crust. When oxygen combines with these elements, it is no longer a gas.

FIND IT

You will be reading about elements throughout this book. Look over the **Periodic Table of Elements** on this page and see how many of the following common elements you can identify by their symbols: O, Si, Fe, H, He, Na, Mg, Al, C.

PERIODIC TABLE OF ELEMENTS

ATOMIC NUMBER — 8
CHEMICAL SYMBOL — O
ELEMENT NAME — OXYGEN

1 **H** HYDROGEN																	2 **He** HELIUM
3 **Li** LITHIUM 6.941	4 **Be** BERYLIUM											5 **B** BORON	6 **C** CARBON	7 **N** NITROGEN	8 **O** OXYGEN	9 **F** FLUORINE	10 **Ne** NEON
11 **Na** SODIUM	12 **Mg** MAGNESIUM											13 **Al** ALUMINUM	14 **Si** SILICON	15 **P** PHOSPHORUS	16 **S** SULFUR	17 **Cl** CHLORINE	18 **Ar** ARGON
19 **K** POTASSIUM	20 **Ca** CALCIUM	21 **Sc** SCANDIUM	22 **Ti** TITANIUM	23 **V** VANADIUM	24 **Cr** CHROMIUM	25 **Mn** MANGANESE	26 **Fe** IRON	27 **Co** COBALT	28 **Ni** NICKEL	29 **Cu** COPPER	30 **Zn** ZINC	31 **Ga** GALLIUM	32 **Ge** GERMANIUM	33 **As** ARSENIC	34 **Se** SELENIUM	35 **Br** BROMINE	36 **Kr** KRYPTON
37 **Rb** RUBIDIUM	38 **Sr** STRONTIUM	39 **Y** YTTRIUM	40 **Zr** ZIRCONIUM	41 **Nb** NIOBIUM	42 **Mo** MOLYBDENUM	43 **Tc** TECHNETIUM	44 **Ru** RUTHENIUM	45 **Rh** RHODIUM	46 **Pd** PALLADIUM	47 **Ag** SILVER	48 **Cd** CADMIUM	49 **In** INDIUM	50 **Sn** TIN	51 **Sb** ANTIMONY	52 **Te** TELLURIUM	53 **I** IODINE	54 **Xe** XENON
55 **Cs** CESIUM	56 **Ba** BARIUM		72 **Hf** HAFNIUM	73 **Ta** TANTALUM	74 **W** TUNGSTEN	75 **Re** RHENIUM	76 **Os** OSMIUM	77 **Ir** IRIDIUM	78 **Pt** PLATINUM	79 **Au** GOLD	80 **Hg** MERCURY	81 **Tl** THALLIUM	82 **Pb** LEAD	83 **Bi** BISMUTH	84 **Po** POLONIUM	85 **At** ASTATINE	86 **Rn** RADON
87 **Fr** FRANCIUM	88 **Ra** RADIUM		104 **Unq** UNNILQUADIUM	105 **Unp** UNNILPENTIUM	106 **Unh** UNNILHEXIUM	107 **Uns** UNNILSEPTIUM	108 **Uno** UNNILOCTIUM	109 **Une** UNNILENNIUM									

57 **La** LANTHANUM	58 **Ce** CERIUM	59 **Pr** PRASEODYMIUM	60 **Nd** NEODYMIUM	61 **Pm** PROMETHIUM	62 **Sm** SAMARIUM	63 **Eu** EUROPIUM	64 **Gd** GADOLINIUM	65 **Tb** TERBIUM	66 **Dy** DYSPROSIUM	67 **Ho** HOLMIUM	68 **Er** ERBIUM	69 **Tm** THULIUM	70 **Yb** YTTERBIUM	71 **Lu** LUTETIUM
89 **Ac** ACTINIUM	90 **Th** THORIUM	91 **Pa** PROTACTINIUM	92 **U** URANIUM	93 **Np** NEPTUNIUM	94 **Pu** PLUTONIUM	95 **Am** AMERICIUM	96 **Cm** CURIUM	97 **Bk** BERKELIUM	98 **Cf** CALIFORNIUM	99 **Es** EINSTEINIUM	100 **Fm** FERMIUM	101 **Md** MENDELEVIUM	102 **No** NOBELIUM	103 **Lr** LAWRENCIUM

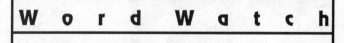

W o r d W a t c h

The word **element** comes from the Latin word **elementum**, which referred to the four basic substances that the ancient Romans felt composed the universe — fire, water, earth, and air. To this date, 109 basic substances that compose the matter of the universe have been identified. We still use the word "element" to describe them.

The first table of elements, published in 1789 in a textbook written by a French chemist, had only 21 elements. Scientists have since discovered 88 more.

Chapter 3

The Lithosphere

Not all of the planets in our Solar System have a solid outer crust. Some planets are not solid — they are composed mainly of gases. That is why you cannot go for a walk on the planet Jupiter. Jupiter is a gaseous planet with no firm surface area. There will never be roads or hiking trails on the surface of Jupiter.

The planet Earth is different from Jupiter and the planets that have orbits beyond Jupiter. Earth is one of the four planets closest to the Sun, and all of these planets are called **solid planets.**

In this chapter, we will explore the solid planet Earth. We will explore its deepest trenches and climb its highest mountain peaks. Our journey begins at the center of the Earth.

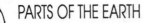

Parts of the Earth

In what way is an apple like our Earth?

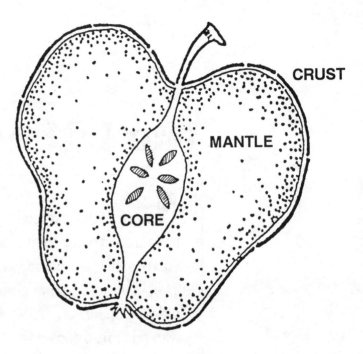

Inside and Out

Pretend the Earth is an apple that you have cut in half. In the center of the apple you will discover a core. The Earth has a **core**, too. It is divided into two parts — the **inner core** and the **outer core**. Both of these cores are made of the elements iron (Fe) and nickel (Ni). The inner core, at the very center of the Earth, is solid. The outer core, just outside the inner core, is molten iron and nickel. These two cores together are 2,200 miles (3,350 km) thick.

The flesh of the apple is like the middle, or **mantle**, of the Earth. The mantle is made of thick, solid rock that contains the following elements: silicon (Si), oxygen (O), aluminum (Al), iron (Fe), and magnesium (Mg). The mantle is 1,800 miles (2,900 km) thick.

Above the mantle is the part of the Earth that is the easiest to investigate — the **crust**. It is made of oxygen (O), silicon (Si), and aluminum (Al). The crust of the Earth is like the skin of the apple: it is very thin in comparison to the rest of the Earth. Even though the crust is thin, it is still thick enough that scientists cannot drill through it into the mantle. The average thickness of the crust is 5 to 25 miles (8 to 40 km).

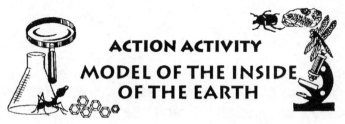

ACTION ACTIVITY
MODEL OF THE INSIDE OF THE EARTH

Make your own model to show the three layers inside the Earth: the crust, the mantle, and the core.

MATERIALS
- **a Styrofoam ball**
- **pencil**
- **markers or crayons**
- **4 feet (121.9 cm) of string or yarn**
- **small hairpin**
- **white glue**

1. Have an adult help you cut a section or ¼ wedge out of the Styrofoam ball, as illustrated.

2. Use a pencil to draw the Earth's layers inside the ball. Look at the illustration to see how thick to make these layers. Color the layers with markers or crayons.

3. Color the outside of the ball blue. Draw and color small land masses and glue them around the outside of the model, or draw the land directly on the Styrofoam ball. Color the land brown.

4. Loop one end of the string through the hairpin and tie it in place. Push the pin into the top of your model. Pull the pin out, fill the hole formed with glue, and push the pin back into the space. Allow to dry for several hours before hanging it from the ceiling.

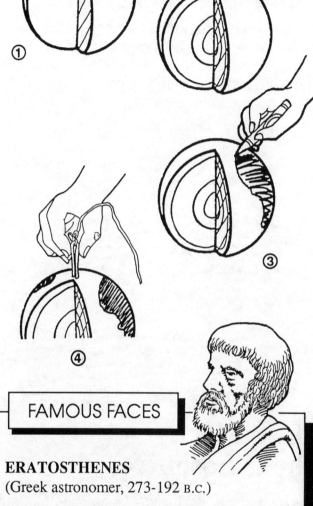

Here is how the thickness of the Earth's crust compares with other distances. If an average person walked 1½ hours, the distance walked (5 miles or 8 km) would be equal to the thickness of the crust under the ocean. If a person drove 30 minutes at 55 mph (88 kph), the distance traveled would equal the thickness of the continental crust (approximately 25 miles or 40 km).

FAMOUS FACES

ERATOSTHENES
(Greek astronomer, 273-192 B.C.)

More than 2,000 years ago, while working as the librarian of the Library of Alexandria, Egypt, Eratosthenes figured out how to calculate the **circumference** (distance around the outside) of the Earth. His calculations were amazingly accurate: his figure was 28,721 miles (45,954 km). The actual circumference is 25,000 miles (40,000 km)!

Earth's Crust

When we talk about the crust of the Earth, it sounds like we are ordering a pizza, because there are two kinds of crust—thick and thin. The rock that forms the continents is granite, and the rock that forms the ocean floor is basalt. These rocks form the thick and thin crust of Earth.

Thick and Thin Crust

The thick layer that forms the continents is called the **sial** layer. That is because it is made mainly of the elements silicon (Si) and aluminum (Al). The word "sial" is formed by putting together the first two letters of the names of these elements.

The thin layer under the thick layer of the continents also forms the ocean floor. It is called the **sima** layer. Can you guess the main elements that form this layer? Silicon (Si) and magnesium (Mg) form this layer.

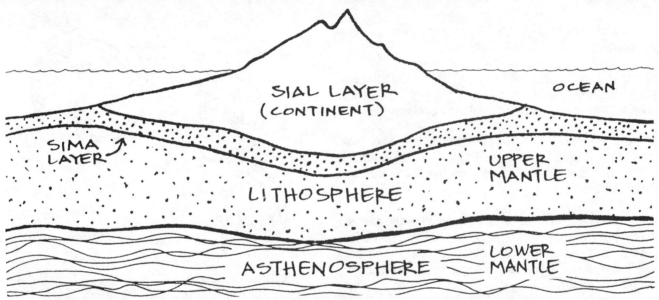

The Surface: The Lithosphere

The thick sial and thin sima layers together form what we call the **crust**. Together with the upper, solid layer of the **mantle**, they form the thick, solid, outer shell of the Earth, called the **lithosphere**. Although we normally cannot feel it, the lithosphere is slowly and constantly moving. The continents sit on top of the lithosphere and are carried with it as it floats on top of the partially molten layer of the upper mantle, called the **asthenosphere.**

Under the Surface: The Asthenosphere

The asthenosphere is made of melted rock, or **magma**, mixed with solid chunks of rock. This is where the magma originates that works its way into the lithosphere to form new crust.

The asthenosphere, because it is partially molten, is flexible. The heat within the asthenosphere and the heat from the hotter layers below it cause it to move slowly around the Earth. Because the lithosphere sits on top of the asthenosphere, the lithosphere is moved at the same time.

ACTION ACTIVITY
A BALANCING ACT

The continental crust and the ocean crust are balanced on top of the flexible lithosphere and the fluid asthenosphere. These balancing movements are known as **isostasy**. In this activity you can see how this balancing act, or isostasy, occurs.

MATERIALS
• balance scale
• loose dirt or sand
• 2 cake pans or pie plates
• two spiral notebooks the same size or two thin books the same size

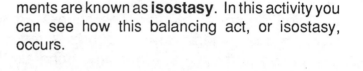

1. The balance scale represents the asthenosphere. Place one notebook on each side of the scale. (See the illustration.)

2. The notebooks represent the crust of the Earth. Move them until the scale is balanced.

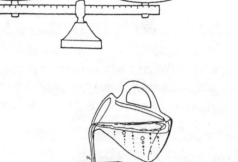

3. Place the pans on top of each notebook. Fill one pan half full of water. This represents the Earth's ocean.

4. Place enough sand or dirt in the other pan to balance the dirt with the water. Mound the dirt up like a mountain. This represents Earth's land.

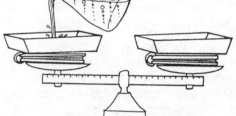

5. Remove a spoonful of dirt and place it in the water.

Watch what happens. Does the land pan rise and the water pan sink lower? This is what happens to the Earth's crust.

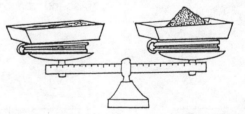

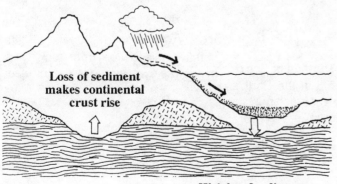

Loss of sediment
makes continental
crust rise

Weight of sediment
pushes down ocean crust

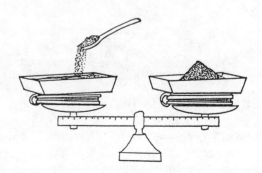

Rocks and Minerals: Gifts of the Crust

The Earth's crust is made of layers of rocks. All rocks are made from matter called **minerals**, and minerals are made of different combinations of elements. The sand we find at the beach is made of the mineral quartz. Quartz is made of the elements silicon (Si) and oxygen (O). Some minerals, like copper (Cu), silver (Ag), gold (Au), and tin (Sn) are pure; they are each made of only one type of element.

Cu

Ag

Au

Sn

Rocks and Minerals in History Timeline

The rocks and minerals that form the crust of the Earth have been collected by mankind since early times and have been used to make artworks, tools, weapons, religious objects, and jewelry. The history of the human race is divided into periods of time based upon the use of the Earth's rocks and minerals. These time periods tell the story of civilization.

Stone Age: Around half a million years ago, the earliest humans found that certain rocks, like flint and obsidian, could be chipped into crude blades and axe heads, making it easier to hunt and skin animals for food, clothing, and shelter. ➡

Copper Age: Around 6000 B.C., the first metal mineral, copper, was discovered and used for making tools, utensils, and weapons. ➡

Bronze Age: Around 3000 B.C., it was discovered that mixing tin (Sn) with copper (Cu) forms bronze, a metal stronger than copper. Armies with bronze weapons could easily defeat armies with copper weapons. ⬇

Industrial Age: The Age of Factories. Fuels discovered in the Earth's crust are used to power machinery.
Age of Coal and Steam —1750
Age of Oil —1850
Age of Uranium —The "Atomic Age" —1950's
⬅

Iron Age: Around 2000 B.C., Hittite nomads mined iron from rock. This metal was even stronger than bronze. ⬅

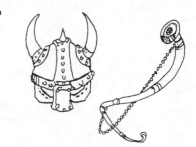

Information Age: The Age of Computers (Present)
Age of Silicon —1980: Silicon is used to make computer chips. Silicon chips are now found in everything from cars to airplanes to video games.

ACTION ACTIVITY
COLLECTING AND
IDENTIFYING ROCKS

Starting a rock collection is a fun way to begin identifying our "gifts" from the Earth's crust.

MATERIALS
- **backpack or sack**
- **thick hand towel or rag (optional)**
- **small hammer (optional)**
- **safety glasses (optional)**
- **very light-colored fingernail polish**
- **black permanent ink marker**
- **notebook**

1. Begin your rock collection by looking for rocks along river banks, plowed fields, highway cuts, beaches, and places where soil is being moved for a building. Look for rocks as you visit other areas of your city, or travel to other towns or states.

2. Look for small rocks or, with an adult's OK, you can break off small pieces of large rocks for your collection by doing the following: Wearing your safety glasses, cover the rock to be broken with a thick towel or rag. Hit the covered rock with the hammer until it breaks into smaller pieces. (NEVER break a rock unless you are wearing safety glasses and the rock is covered with a cloth. This will prevent chips from cutting you or damaging your eyes.)

3. Group your rocks into boxes by their similarities. Look at color, shape, and texture. You might have boxes with the following labels: flat rocks; smooth, round rocks; rocks that break easily; rocks with crystals; and so on. You can use egg cartons to group and store your smaller rocks.

4. Check out a library book that will help you name your rocks. As you name your rocks, paint a spot of fingernail polish on each rock. Allow this to dry. With the black marker, write a number on top of the fingernail polish. Record the rock's number and name in a notebook.

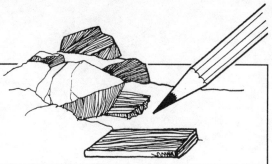

The "lead" in your pencil is not really the element lead (Pb). It is the mineral graphite, which is the element carbon (C). The graphite is mixed with clay to make pencil leads that are either soft or hard.

Naming Rocks

As we collect rocks, we discover they do not all look and feel the same. Some of the rocks are smooth and shiny, while others are rough like sandpaper. Some break easily, while others are so strong they can cut glass. There are so many different types of rocks, how do we begin to name them?

Three Basic Types of Rocks

Rocks are formed in three basic ways. One way to name rocks is after the way they were formed: **igneous, sedimentary,** or **metamorphic.**

Sedimentary rock is formed by layers of **sediments**. Sediments are loose materials deposited together by water, wind, or glacial ice. Examples of sediments are sand, mud, and bits of broken-down rock. Sedimentary rock is formed by layers of sediments piling up on top of each other over thousands of years. The weight of all the top layers of new sediment causes the bottom layers to bond, or "glue," together to form solid rock. Sandstone, limestone, and mudstone are sedimentary rocks. Can you tell by their names what sediments they are made of?

Some sedimentary rocks are made of parts of animals and plants. For example, limestone is made of many shells and skeletons of small marine animals that died and drifted to the bottom of their water habitat. The animals' remains were mixed with silt and mineral sediments, and after thousands of years and many layers of sediment, limestone was formed.

Coal is made from layers of compressed plant material. If you look closely at a piece of bituminous coal (not charcoal) you can see the compressed layers. Bituminous coal is a sedimentary rock that can be burned as fuel.

Sedimentary rock is easy to find. Three out of four rocks found on the Earth's surface are sedimentary. You can see layers of sedimentary rock where highways cut through hills, in cliffs, and where rivers cut through the land, forming canyons such as the Grand Canyon in Arizona.

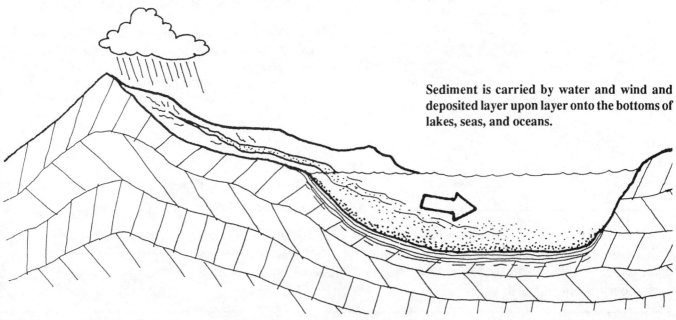

Sediment is carried by water and wind and deposited layer upon layer onto the bottoms of lakes, seas, and oceans.

Igneous rock is formed from **magma** (very hot liquid rock found in the mantle) that works its way into the crust below the Earth's surface, where it cools and hardens. When magma breaks through to the surface of the crust, it is then called **lava**. Volcanoes bring magma to the surface of the Earth. Most of the lava that reaches the crust is from volcanoes. When lava cools and hardens, it also forms igneous rock.

Granite is the most common igneous rock. It forms the continents. Basalt is an igneous rock that covers the whole surface of the Earth beneath the oceans and the continents. Obsidian and pumice are examples of other common igneous rocks.

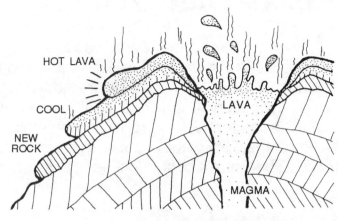

Formation of igneous rock

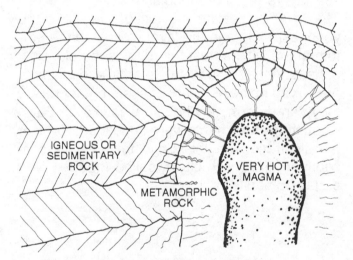

Formation of metamorphic rock

Metamorphic rock is igneous or sedimentary rock that has been changed into a different kind of rock by extreme heat and pressure. Metamorphic rocks are formed below the surface of the crust when igneous or sedimentary rock becomes heated by magma, or when rocks get squeezed and pressed together in the intense heat and pressure that occurs during the formation of mountains.

Under extreme heat and pressure, limestone, a sedimentary rock, turns into marble, a metamorphic rock. Shale and clay, both sedimentary rocks, turn into slate. Sandstone turns into schist.

Where to Find Them

Over 90% of the rocks deep under the Earth's surface are igneous or metamorphic. Most of the rocks on the surface are sedimentary. Can you figure out why? It's because heat and pressure are needed to form igneous rock and metamorphic rock. As these rocks are exposed at the Earth's surface, they are broken down, and the resulting sediment becomes the sedimentary rocks of the Earth's surface.

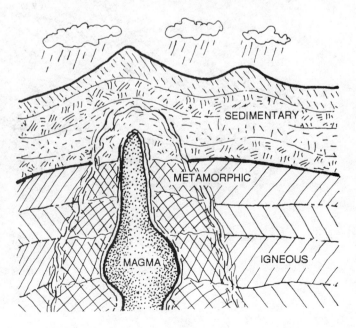

Rocks That "Talk"

How do we know what Earth was like millions of years ago? How do we know what life on Earth was like throughout time? The answers to these questions are hidden in the Earth itself. In our investigation of the Earth's lithosphere, we have learned about the different kinds of rocks and minerals that form the crust. We know that 75% of the upper crust is composed of sedimentary rocks. The Earth's past is locked in this sedimentary rock.

Locked in Rock

As sediment collects at the bottom of rivers, lakes, and oceans, the remains of dead plants and animals are deposited within the sediment. For example, as layer after layer of sediment is deposited on the ocean floor, a record of ocean life is trapped in the sediment. The oldest, or first, life is found in the deepest layer of sediment. Sometimes the oldest rocks, the ones that were very deep, are brought closer to the surface of the crust by erosion and uplift. When this happens, fossil clues once hidden in the depths of the Earth are exposed at the surface for us to discover.

When a highway is cut through a hill, you might see layers of different-colored rock in the hill. The layer closest to the top of the hill is the youngest rock, and the layer closest to the bottom of the hill, nearest the road, is the oldest.

As scientists study the plants and animals preserved in these layers of sedimentary rocks, they can determine what life was like on Earth when these sediments were deposited. Look at the illustration on this page to see layers of sediment filled with clues, called **fossils**. (See pages 38 and 39.)

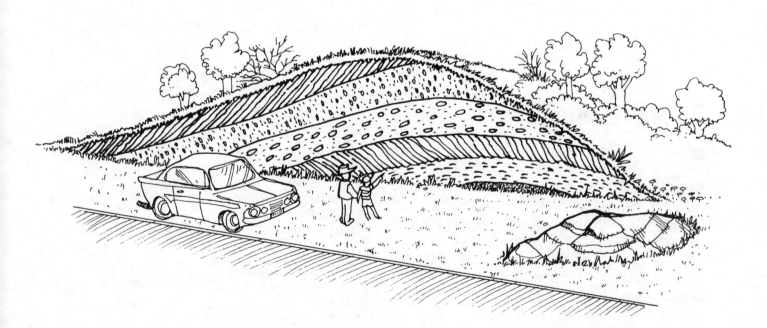

ACTION ACTIVITY
MAKING AND BREAKING A ROCK

Rocks that are formed under the Earth's surface break down when they are brought to the surface of the Earth and exposed to the elements.

MATERIALS

- 1 cup (250 ml) of sand
- ½ cup (125 ml) of water
- large paper cup
- ½ cup (125 ml) plaster of Paris

1. Mix the plaster with the sand in the paper cup.

2. Add ½ cup (125 ml) water, and stir. If the mixture is too thick to stir, add a little more water. If you add too much water, punch a small hole in the bottom of the cup and allow the extra water to drain out into an old pan.

3. Allow the mixture to dry overnight. Carefully remove the paper cup.

You have made artificial sandstone.

4. Place your "sandstone" rock outside in a location where it will not be disturbed, but where it will be exposed to the weather. Watch what happens to your rock over a period of several months.

Watch closely for any changes in its shape.

The next time you eat a chocolate chip cookie, think of it as sandstone or mudstone filled with clues to the past. The "fossils" (chips) embedded in the "rock" (cookie) are fragile and difficult to remove. Use a toothpick to remove one of the "fossils." You have to remove the surrounding "rock" very carefully to keep from harming the "fossil." With an adult helper, digging tools, and brushes, you can use this same process to remove a fossil from rock.

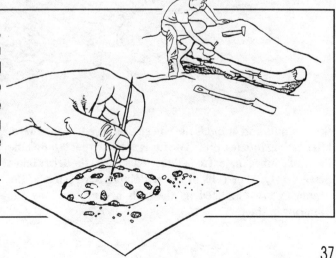

Fossil Formation

If you took an old Christmas tree and placed it in a location where it would not be disturbed for millions of years, would it become a fossil? When a plant or animal dies, it decays or rots. This decaying process returns basic elements to the Earth. This is what will happen to the Christmas tree. So what can you do to make the conditions right for this tree to be preserved as a fossil clue?

The Making of a Fossil

Fossils are formed when plants or animals die and are immediately covered by sediment, mud, or sand. When covered, the organisms that cause the decay, decomposers like **bacteria** (see pages 98 and 99), are not able to work as quickly. They need oxygen to work, and the sediment limits the amount of oxygen available. A special kind of bacteria, called **anaerobic** bacteria, or bacteria that can work without oxygen, begin to decompose the dead organism.

Anaerobic bacteria work very slowly. As bacteria break down the soft tissue of the plant or animal, the harder parts of the organism remain. For animals, these parts are usually the bones,

teeth, claws, shells, and scales. Muscle, skin, and other body parts that are made out of soft cells decay too quickly to fossilize. In plants, it is often the leaves, stems, or wood that remain. Plants have very strong cells that are made of cellulose, and this tough material makes it easier for plants to be preserved whole.

The organism is held in the sediment. As the decaying takes place, water moves through the sediment. One of the properties of water is that it is able to dissolve minerals. The minerals dissolved in the water collect in the decayed cells of the plant or animal. Over time, the organism is replaced by the minerals that have collected in the cells.

Some plants and animals have been preserved, or fossilized, after falling into tar pits. The tar is so thick that it limits the amount of oxygen, just as sediment does, and the decay takes place slowly. The cells of the remaining hard parts of the organism are fossilized as the cells are replaced by the minerals in the tar.

Molds and Casts

Sometimes when an organism is trapped in sediment, it decays slowly and its cells are not replaced with minerals. The result is called a **mold**. It is a hollow space that is shaped like the organism.

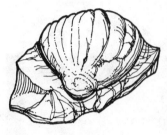

Sometimes after a mold is formed, water passes through the mold and deposits minerals into the hollow space. The space becomes filled, and the result is a fossil called a **cast**. It does not have the same cell structure as the original organism; it is just a filled-in mold.

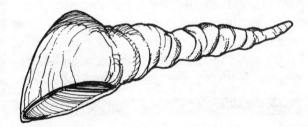

Many office buildings are made of blocks cut from quarries of sedimentary rock. Examine rock blocks in your area, and you might find cast and mold fossils on public display.

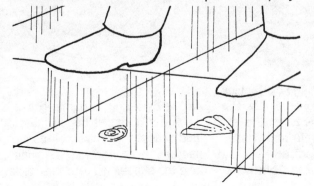

ACTION ACTIVITY
MAKE A FOSSIL

In this activity you will make a mold fossil and a cast fossil that will fit together like a puzzle.

MATERIALS
- object from nature — chicken bone, twig, or shell
- ½ cup (125 ml) of plaster of Paris
- ¼ cup (62.5 ml) of water
- petroleum jelly
- small, clean plastic butter dish

1. Cover the nature object with petroleum jelly.

2. Pour the water into the butter dish. Pour the plaster of Paris into the water and allow it to sit without stirring for three minutes.

3. Press the nature object into the plaster and allow the plaster to dry. This will take about 24 hours. The plaster will look like white chalk when it is dry.

4. Remove the object from the plaster. You have a mold of your nature object.

5. Leave the dry plaster mold in the butter dish and cover it with petroleum jelly. Pour another mixture of plaster over the mold and allow this to dry.

6. When the second layer of plaster is dry, it will separate from the mold along the layer of petroleum jelly and you will see a cast.

These examples will help you identify mold and cast fossils in the world around you.

Plate Tectonics: A Giant Earth Puzzle

Have you ever tried to put a jigsaw puzzle together? Usually, the larger the puzzle pieces, the easier the puzzle is to assemble. However, this is not always true. For hundreds of years, geographers wondered why the continents looked like giant puzzle pieces that had been pulled apart. They couldn't explain how or why the continents were shaped the way they were. It was a giant puzzle.

Drifting Away

Now scientists believe in the theory originally proposed by Alfred Wegener (see box) that the continents were once one large land mass that has gradually split apart over millions of years.

Wegener's "wandering continents" theory is also called by many other names. **Continental drift** and **plate tectonics** are the most common. It does not matter what it is called; what matters is what happened and what continues to happen on the Earth during these movements.

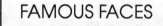

FAMOUS FACES

ALFRED WEGENER
(German astronomer, 1880-1930)

In 1911, a German scientist named Alfred Wegener tried to explain the puzzle-piece continents. His "wandering continents" theory proposed that at one time all of the continents were connected into one giant super-continent. As time passed, the continents slowly moved apart. People were shocked at this thought, and Alfred Wegener's theory was ignored until the 1960s.

Plate Tectonics Timeline

At the beginning of the Age of Reptiles, 225 million years ago when the dinosaurs first walked on Earth, all of the continents formed one giant continent called **Pangaea**. The waters of the Earth formed one giant ocean called **Panthalassa**.

By the middle of the Age of Reptiles, when the giant dinosaurs like Diplodocus walked on the Earth, the land divided into two separate land masses: the northern land, called **Laurasia,** and the southern land, called **Gondwana**.

As the dinosaurs became extinct and the Age of Mammals began, most of the land masses we now call continents had separated and were beginning to take the shapes we recognize today.

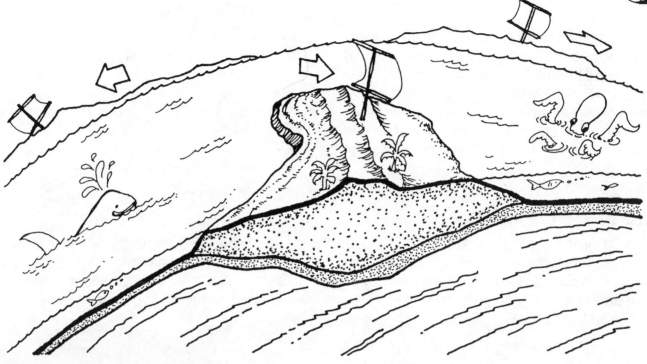

Gathering Proof

The theory of "wandering continents" has gained popular acceptance. What kind of proof did the scientists need to accept this theory? These facts illustrate some of the "proof" collected by scientists.

- Fossils of similar plants and animals dating back 200 million years were found on different continents. Fossils of Mesosaurus, an aquatic reptile, have been found on the east coast of South America and the west coast of Africa. Fossils of Lystrosaurus, a kind of reptilian hippopotamus, have been found in South Africa, Asia, and Antarctica. Two hundred million years ago, all these continents must have been connected.

- Research was conducted on the magnetic alignment of the oldest rocks on the different continents. This research showed that either the magnetic poles of the Earth had moved or the continents had moved out of their original alignment with these poles.

- Similar rocks and crust formations that date back 200 million years have been found on different continents.

- The discovery that the floor of the Atlantic Ocean is spreading at the Mid-Atlantic ridge, pushing the continents along its boundaries apart by centimeters each year, showed how the plates could be, and are, continually moving. Further proof of this can be seen by examining mineral deposits in South Africa and Argentina. At one time these countries were connected, sharing some of the world's largest diamond deposits. Today these rare deposits can be found in both countries, which are separated by thousands of miles of ocean.

Many Christmas tree ornaments are glass balls. If you were to drop one of these ornaments on a hard floor, it would break into large and small pieces. If you were able to put these pieces together again, you would have an ornament with cracks on its surface. You can picture the crust of the Earth as being like this cracked ornament.

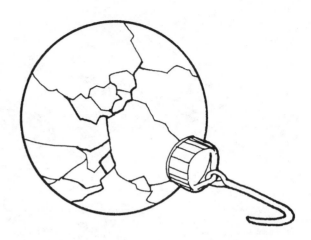

The Major Plates

The crust of the Earth is broken into 13 major pieces, or **plates**, that move with the lithosphere. These plates do not all move in the same way or at the same speed. Because the plates move, the surface of the Earth, little by little, is always changing. The major plates are named on the map below. The arrows show where plates are moving apart or coming together.

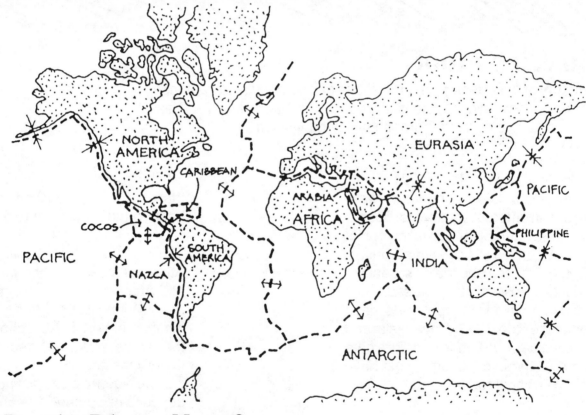

How Do the Plates Move?

Plates move in three ways. They can move apart, crash into each other, or slide past each other. When plates move apart to form a crack, or **rift**, hot molten magma comes to the surface, forming new crust. These areas between plates are called **constructive boundaries** because new crust is "constructed."

When plates collide, the crust is destroyed. The crust of one plate goes under the crust of another plate. This moves the old crust back into the mantle, where it is melted. These areas are called **destructive boundaries** because the crust is remelted and begins a recycling process. Volcanoes often form along destructive boundaries.

Sometimes mountains are formed at plate collision points. The Alps in Switzerland and the Himalayas in India were formed by plate collisions. Millions of years ago, India was a large island that collided with China. This collision caused the soft edges of both plates to crunch upward, forming the Himalayan mountain range, where the tallest mountain in the world, Mount Everest, is found.

Plates can also slide sideways, past each other. This happens along fault lines such as the San Andreas fault in California. When this happens, the lithosphere is not destroyed or created, just moved. This movement can cause earthquakes.

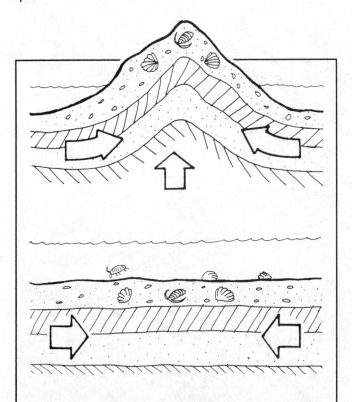

Fossils of fish and shells have been found on the top of the Himalayan mountains. How did they get there? The edges of land masses are made of soft sedimentary rock formed by the dirt and sand that has washed off the land into the water and from the bodies and shells of animals that lived in the water. When land masses collide, this soft rock is pushed upward. What was ocean floor is now the top of this mountain chain.

ACTION ACTIVITY
3-WAY MOTION

Do the following activity to see what happens when the Earth's plates move in three different ways: moving apart, colliding, and sliding past each other.

MATERIALS
• **2 small pieces of foam rubber**

1. Pretend that each piece of foam is a plate forming the Earth's lithosphere. Take the two pieces of foam and place them flat on a table top.

2. Press the two pieces of foam slowly toward each other. What happens when plates come together?

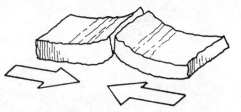

3. Place the two pieces of foam close together on a table so that their sides are touching. Slowly move them apart. How does the surface of the Earth change as plates move?

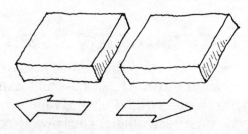

4. Place the two pieces of foam close together on a table so that their sides are touching. Move the plates in opposite directions as their sides touch. What happens when the plates move against each other?

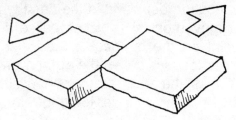

When the Earth Quakes

When the Earth moved on October 17, 1989, during the World Series game in San Francisco, people were terrified. Buildings that once seemed safe and strong cracked and fell. Bridges that people drove over every day became dangerous and unsafe. What had happened to cause this? Why did the Earth move?

An Earthshaking Event

The slow movement of the Earth's plates causes great pressures to build up in the crust, especially along the borders of the plates, where they collide, slide past each other, or pull away from each other. When there is a sudden release of pressure, usually deep within the Earth, the crust shifts in one quick movement, and an **earthquake** occurs.

The location deep within the crust where the sudden movement takes place is called the **focus**. The point on the surface of the crust directly above the focus is called the **epicenter**. As you might guess, the areas that experience the most earthquakes are those located along plate boundaries.

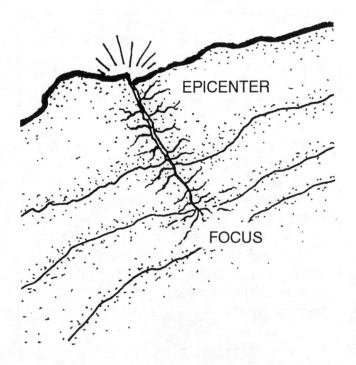

EPICENTER

FOCUS

44

Making Waves

Nearly half a million earthquakes occur each year on the surface of the Earth. Most of these are weak and do not cause damage. Many earthquakes occur along plates on the ocean floor. When the focus of a strong earthquake is under the ocean, the water above the focus is moved. This shifted area of disturbed water can create a giant wave, called a **tsunami** (soo-**na**-mee).

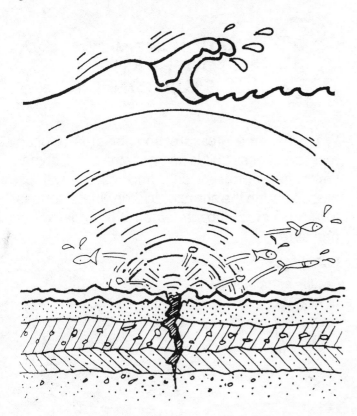

The tsunami moves across the ocean surface, often hitting areas of land, causing great damage and death. Even though these huge waves are sometimes called "tidal waves," they are not influenced by the gravitational pull of the moon, as are tides.

ACTION ACTIVITY
OCEAN EARTHQUAKE

When an earthquake occurs at the bottom of the sea, giant waves (tsunamis) up to 100 miles (160 km) long can rush to the shore at speeds up to 500 miles per hour. At mid-ocean the tsunami may be barely noticeable, but close to shore they may grow to more than 100 feet (30 m) high. Create your own tsunami in a tub or basin.

MATERIALS

- **water**
- **bathtub**
- **two bricks**
- **toy boat (optional)**
- **wax paper** (about 24", or 61 cm, long)
- **string** (2 pieces, about 12", or 30 cm, each)

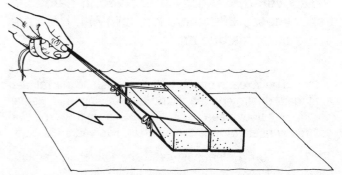

1. Tie a piece of string around each end of one brick. Lay a sheet of wax paper on the bottom of the tub.

2. Place both bricks on top of the wax paper.

3. Fill the tub with water, just covering the bricks by about ¾ inch (2 cm). With a sharp tug, quickly pull the brick with the string to one side. This simulates the movement of the ocean floor during an earthquake.

4. What happens at the surface of the water? This is how a tsunami begins. A toy boat placed over the center of the two bricks will show the effects of a tsunami.

45

Volcanoes

It is a busy workday in Pompeii, a small village in Italy, in the year 79 A.D. Everyone is busy at work and school, when suddenly they hear a loud sound coming from Mount Vesuvius, and the sky begins to darken. Mount Vesuvius, a volcanic mountain, is erupting!

Looking Back

Each volcanic eruption is different, but most volcanoes release gases, lava, rock fragments, and ash from the depths of the Earth. In Pompeii, the Sun was blocked by huge amounts of ash, and people and animals were forced to breathe poisonous sulfur gas fumes released into the air by the volcano. Most of Pompeii's residents died, and the city disappeared under 20 feet (6 m) of volcanic ash. Pompeii and its residents were rediscovered, perfectly preserved in hardened ash, almost 1,800 years later in 1711. Here are some other historic eruptions.

1883 The volcano on the Indonesian island of Krakatau exploded, destroying the island and leaving only a small portion of it above sea level. The dust from the explosion colored sunsets around the Earth for two years.

1902 Mount Pelée destroyed the Caribbean coastal town of St. Pierre on Martinique island, killing all but two of its 28,000 inhabitants. The volcano erupted again later the same year.

1963 The volcano Surtsey—an example of marine volcanic activity—erupted to create a new island in the sea off the coast of Iceland.

1980 When Mount St. Helens erupted in Washington state, winds spread volcanic ash as far away as Oklahoma and Minnesota. The energy of the blast was 1,300 times as powerful as the bomb that destroyed Hiroshima, Japan, during World War II.

1985 The eruption of Nevada del Ruiz in northern Columbia melted snow on its summit, causing a massive mud slide that covered the town of Armero.

1991 After Mt. Pinatubo, in the Philippines, erupted, 36,000 people were evacuated.

ACTION ACTIVITY TOOTHPASTE ERUPTION

When extreme pressure from magma (molten rock) and gases builds up under the crust, sometimes the hot gases, ash, and magma will explode through the surface. Watch what happens to a tube of toothpaste when it is under great pressure.

MATERIALS
• **a tube of toothpaste**
• **a helper**

1. Use a full tube of toothpaste, or press all of the toothpaste to one end of a used tube. The tube represents the lithosphere of the Earth, and the toothpaste inside represents the molten magma under the lithosphere.

2. Continue to press on the tube, causing great pressure on the "magma" inside the tube.

3. Have a helper press a pin into the toothpaste tube while you place the "magma" under pressure. What happens? If the toothpaste container is compared to the crust of the Earth, the erupting toothpaste can be compared to hot magma. Magma is moved by strong heat and pressure. If the magma finds a crack or a fault line in the crust, it erupts through the surface and releases the pressure.

What Happens?

Volcanoes form over very hot spots within the Earth's mantle. These hot spots are often located over **destructive zones**, or areas where crustal plates meet and one plate is forced down below the other plate. This is known as **subduction**. A great deal of heat is created from the friction of the plates moving past each other.

The lower part of the Earth's crust and the upper part of the mantle begin to melt, forming magma. This magma is not as dense as the solid rock that surrounds it, so it begins to rise. If there is a fault line or a weak spot in the crust, the magma begins to move up into these openings, melting the rock around it as it goes, and forming a large pocket of melted rock, called a **magma chamber.**

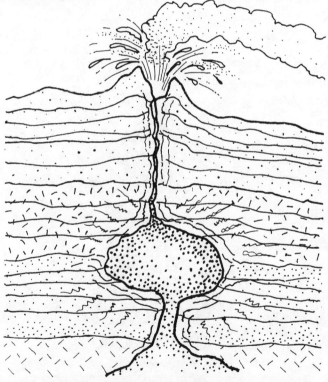

The melting rock releases gases that slowly build up pressure within the chamber. Eventually, the pressure within the chamber gets so high that an explosion, like a giant "burp," occurs, venting the hot gases and magma to the surface of the Earth. When the magma reaches the surface it is called **lava**, and the lava forms a volcanic mountain or plateau.

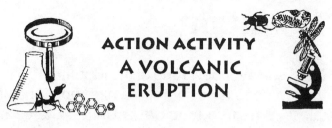

ACTION ACTIVITY A VOLCANIC ERUPTION

When molten rock (magma) reaches the surface, it is then called lava. With this activity you can see what a volcano looks like when it erupts.

MATERIALS
- **sand or dirt**
- **¼ cup (62.5 ml) water**
- **¼ cup (62.5 ml) vinegar**
- **large dishpan or washtub**
- **3 tablespoons dishwashing liquid**
- **several drops red food coloring**
- **tall, thin jar that holds about 1 cup of liquid, and lid**
- **¼ cup (62.5 ml) baking soda (sodium bicarbonate)**

1. Mix the soda, water, and food coloring in the jar.

2. Cover the jar with the lid. Do not screw the lid on too tightly. You will need to be able to remove it easily.

3. Place the jar in the middle of the tub or pan. Pile the loose dirt around the sides of the jar until you have formed a "volcano."

4. Carefully open the lid and remove it from the jar. Quickly pour the vinegar into the jar. What happens?

Mountains

Did you ever play King of the Mountain? The "King" in the game tries to keep a position on a high point that is called the "mountain." When you look at a United States map, it is filled with thousands of areas that have the words "mount" or "mountain" in their name, but many of these locations are not really mountains.

Defining a Mountain

So what exactly is a mountain? Are there any rules as to what a mountain should be? Geographers define a mountain as land that extends at least 2,000 feet (733 meters) above sea level. It is steep, with long slopes, deep canyons, valleys, and ridges. A true mountain will have at least two different areas, or zones, of climate and life. Geologists say that a mountain must have rock layers that are tilted, showing it was formed by folding or faulting. (See illustration below.)

The Making of a Mountain

Mountains are created as the plates of the Earth's crust move. Mountain building is a slow process. It takes thousands of years for a mountain chain to form. There are four main ways in which mountains are made.

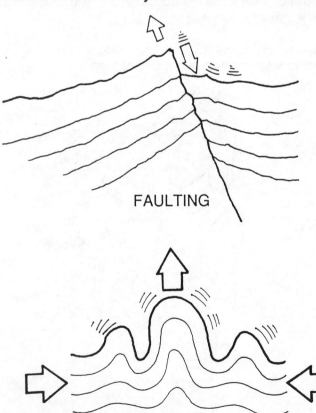

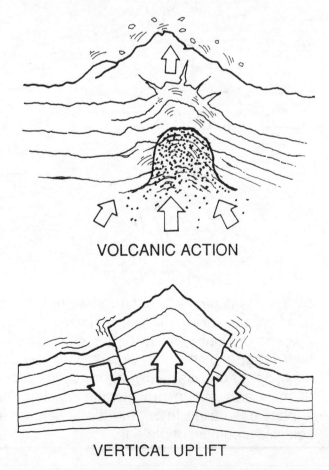

FAULTING

VOLCANIC ACTION

FOLDING

VERTICAL UPLIFT

ACTION ACTIVITY
FOLDING MOUNTAINS

One way mountains are formed is when layers of rocks are pushed into a series of wavelike folds.

MATERIALS
- **3 bath towels**
- **a helper**

1. Fold the towels into long, narrow strips of "land." Stack the towels one on top of another to represent the layers of the Earth.

2. Slowly push the ends of the towels toward the middle.

3. The towels will begin to buckle and fold. This is how many of the mountains on Earth are formed. The land folds in waves because of the pressure and forces caused by the movement of the crust.

FAMOUS FACES

SIR EDMUND HILLARY

(New Zealand explorer, 1919 -   )

A New Zealand mountain climber, Sir Edmund Hillary, became one of the first two men to climb to the top of Mount Everest and return. In 1953, he and a tribesman from Nepal reached the summit. Queen Elizabeth II later knighted him for his achievement. In the late 1950s, Hillary joined a transantarctic expedition to the South Pole. In 1960 he headed an expedition to climb Mount Makalu I, testing man's ability to live without oxygen at high altitudes.

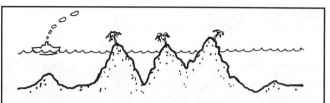

The Hawaiian Islands are **marine mountains** that rise above the water line to form islands.

ACTION ACTIVITY
FIRST MOUNTAINS

Some mountains were formed millions of years ago when the Earth cooled. The mountains resulted from the same type of cooling action that you will see occur in a baked apple.

MATERIALS
- **an apple**
- **a kitchen oven or a toaster oven**
- **an ovenproof plate or flat pan**
- **an adult helper**

1. Preheat the oven to 350°F.

2. Place the apple on the plate or pan.

3. Have the adult helper place the apple in the oven and bake it for 15 minutes.

4. Ask the adult helper to help you remove the apple from the oven, using pot holders. Allow it to cool slowly.

5. Watch what happens to the skin of the apple as the apple cools.

Many scientists think that as the newly formed Earth cooled and the molecules of the matter inside the Earth condensed, the lighter elements forming the crust buckled and moved, forming the first mountains, valleys, and deep ocean floors. Compare the skin of the cooling apple to the crust of the cooling Earth.

Erosion

If you were to dig deep into the Earth's crust, find an ancient igneous rock, and place the rock on the surface of the Earth, this hard rock would begin to change. When exposed to the Earth's atmosphere over millions of years, the rock would be broken down into smaller pieces of rock that would then break down into even smaller pieces of rock that would become sand and possibly even silt. These smaller pieces of rock would be carried away to other parts of the Earth.

Rocks are constantly being broken down into smaller pieces. This process is called **weathering**. When the broken pieces of the rock are carried away or moved by wind, water, or ice, it is called **erosion**.

Let's look at the two kinds of weathering that work at wearing down the surface of the Earth: **chemical** and **physical** changes.

CHEMICAL CHANGES

- Carbonic Acid—"acid rain" (carbon dioxide gas dissolved in water)
- Chemicals added to the atmosphere, water, and soil by humans
- Lichens

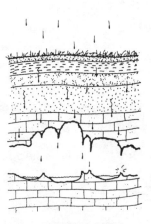

ACID RAIN

CARBONIC ACID
IN GROUNDWATER
DISSOLVES LIMESTONE

LICHENS

PHYSICAL CHANGES

- Rain
- Wind with rock particles
- Water with rock particles
- Constant heating and cooling
- Ice (frost and glaciers)
- Plants (their roots)
- Animals (burrowing)

WIND

CONTRACTION

EXPANSION

BURROWING ANIMALS

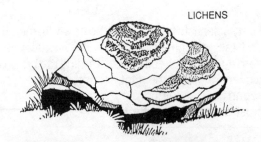

ACTION ACTIVITY
WIND, WATER, AND WEATHERING

See how natural forces such as wind and water cause erosion of the Earth's surfaces.

MATERIALS NEEDED
- hair dryer
- watering can
- pitcher of water
- sand or dirt
- long, flat baking pan
- several small- and medium-sized rocks

If possible, work outside near an electrical outlet.

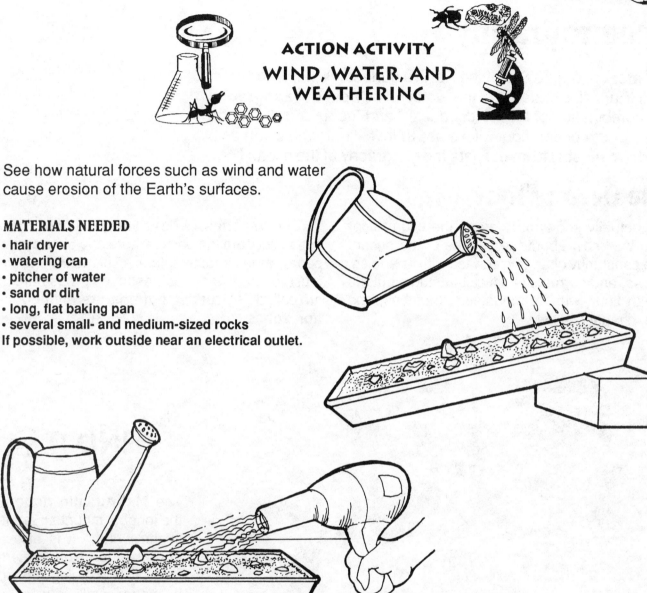

1. Place enough sand or dirt in the pan to cover the bottom evenly, 1 inch (2.5 cm) deep. This forms "land."

2. Carefully plug in the hair dryer. Turn it to the lowest setting to create "wind." Keep the hair dryer 2 feet (60 cm) away from the pan and point the "wind" toward the "land." What happens?

3. Slowly move the "wind" closer to the "land." Is the "wind" moving the soil? Turn the dryer to a higher speed and see what happens to the "land."

4. Place rocks on top of the "land." As the "wind" blows over the "land," what happens to the soil around and under the rocks? Remove the rocks when you are finished.

5. Using the watering can, sprinkle a small amount of water over the "land." Watch closely as the water hits the "land." What happens? Does it change the surface of the "land"?

6. Place a book or block under one end of the pan. Sprinkle more water on the "land." Does the angle of the "land" affect the erosion? Raise the "land" higher and try this again.

7. Place the pan flat on the table. Allow a strong "wind" to blow over the wet "land." How does water affect wind erosion?

8. Create your own erosion activities. For example, try growing grass or other plants in the "land." How does this affect erosion?

51

Oceanography

Water covers 70.8% of the Earth's surface. What is the crust of the Earth like under all of this water? The word **oceanography** is a combination of the words "ocean" and "geography." It is the study of the ocean floor. If we are to investigate the Earth as a solid, we must also investigate the geography of the ocean floor.

The Ocean Floor

We actually know more about the ocean floor than we know about the surface of the ocean. The constantly changing surface with its eddies, waves, and currents is difficult to study, but the ocean floor, with its mountains, trenches, and rifts, changes slowly.

The **trenches**, or deep valleys, found on the ocean floor are the points where one plate disappears under another plate. This is where the crust, or lithosphere, is destroyed. These areas are called **destructive boundaries,** or **subduction zones**.

 **FIND IT**

The **Mid-Atlantic ridge** is the longest mountain range in the world. It is also a **construction zone** where new crust is being formed by magma welling up to the surface from the asthenosphere. Look at the map and find the three main construction ridges on the ocean floor.

The deepest trench is the Mariana Trench located in the eastern part of the Pacific Ocean. It is the deepest point on the Earth, 36,400 feet (11,033 meters) below sea level. Mt. Everest, at 29,000 feet (8,843 m) high, could be buried in the trench and the top of the mountain would still be over 7,000 feet (210 m) below the surface of the ocean!

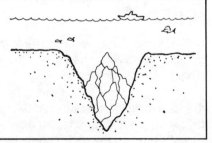

The World's Great Ocean

Although we have many different names for oceans, the Earth really has only one giant ocean. Its waters mix and flow as they are moved by currents, tides, and waves. Oceanographers have divided the world's ocean into different regions that can be named. This makes it easier to talk about certain areas within the ocean. There are three to five (depending on which map you use) large ocean regions that make up the world's ocean.

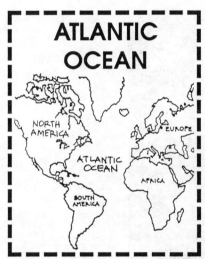

ATLANTIC OCEAN

The **Atlantic Ocean** is the ocean that separates the American continents from the continents of Africa and Europe. The Mid-Atlantic ridge is located here.

The **Pacific Ocean** is the largest and the deepest of all the oceans. There are more volcanoes and islands in this ocean than in any other. It also has the deepest trench, the Mariana Trench.

PACIFIC OCEAN

INDIAN OCEAN

The **Indian Ocean** is the smallest and the shallowest of the three main oceans. The saltiest region of water, the Red Sea, and the warmest region of water, the Persian Gulf, are part of the Indian Ocean.

Some maps label oceans around the arctic regions of the Earth. The **Arctic Ocean** and the **Antarctic Ocean** refer to the waters that surround these polar regions. They are the only regions of the world's ocean that are covered by ice most of the time.

The land that extends out from a continent into the Earth's ocean is called the **continental shelf**. When the shelf begins to angle downward, it is called the **continental slope**. The slope extends to the ocean floor. If we were to look at a section of the ocean connected to a large land mass, this is what it would look like.

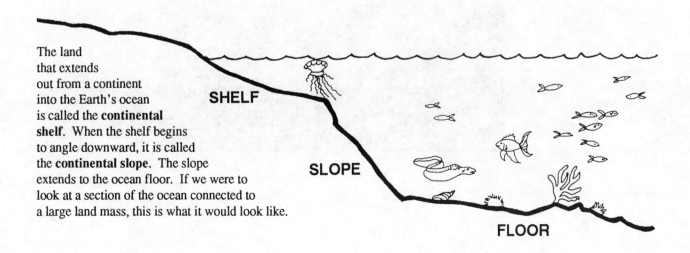

SHELF

SLOPE

FLOOR

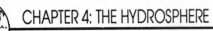

Chapter 4

The Hydrosphere

All living things have something in common with fish: they have to have liquid water to live. There are more plants and animals living in water than out of water, but even those that live on land must continue to "drink" water to stay alive.

Water makes up more than half of the body tissue of all plants and animals. Our bodies are 65% water, an elephant's is 70%, an earthworm's is 80%, and a tomato is 95% water.

Meteorologists, oceanographers, biologists, zoologists, botanists, ecologists, and geologists are just a few of the scientists who study **hydrology**, or how water is involved in Earth's processes. Let's be hydrologists, and investigate what this world is like.

The Three States of Water

Earth is a very unusual planet, because it is the only place where water is found as a solid, liquid, and gas all at the same time. Liquid water enables Earth to have life, but solid water (ice) and gaseous water (vapor) are important, too. These three states of water take part in nearly every process on the face of the earth.

Do you swim? Take a shower? Eat soup? Drink milk? Keep fish in an aquarium? All of these things require LIQUID water. Earth is often called "the water planet," and it is the only planet in the Solar System with liquid water. There is more liquid water on the Earth than any other substance. It fills the world ocean and covers 70.8% of the Earth's surface. Liquid water is needed for life to exist on Earth.

Do you put ice in your drinks? Eat ice cream? Ski? Build snowmen? All of these things require FROZEN water. When water is frozen, it becomes a solid. Frozen water is found around the polar regions of the Earth. Icecaps and glaciers are common. During winter, snow and ice are seen in many of the colder regions of the Earth. Mankind has invented methods for making ice, keeping food cold, and producing snow. Ice and refrigeration are very recent luxuries for everyday life on Earth.

Do you eat hot food? Drink hot chocolate? Take a hot shower? See your breath on a cold day? All of these things produce water VAPOR. The air around us has water in it. When water is a gas, it is called **water vapor**. Water vapor is present in the lower part of the Earth's atmosphere, or air. When you watch clouds move across the sky, you are looking at water vapor.

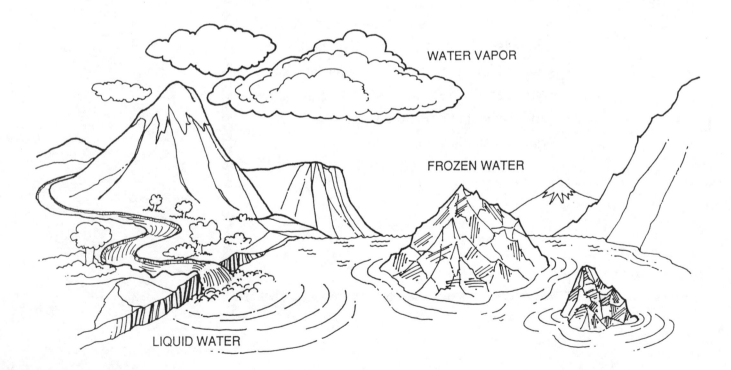

WATER VAPOR

FROZEN WATER

LIQUID WATER

The three phases of water on Earth.

Water Molecules

A water molecule is made of two atoms of hydrogen and one atom of oxygen. This is written as H_2O. Look at the water molecules pictured below as they form ice, liquid, and vapor. What happens to the molecules? Does this explain why the states of matter are so different?

Solid

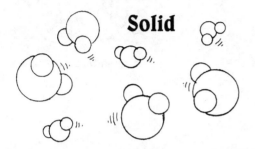

Water molecules are always moving. If they are moving slowly and slightly away from each other, the water is close to freezing. When they nearly stop moving, the water freezes.

Liquid

If the molecules are close together, but moving around freely, the water is liquid.

Vapor

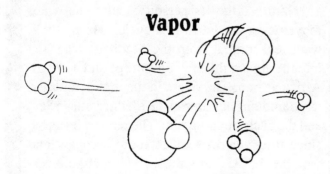

When water is a vapor, or gas, the molecules are farthest apart and move about quickly, constantly bouncing off each other.

ACTION ACTIVITY
100 CUPS OF WATER

If you fill 100 cups with water to represent all the water (100%) on Earth, you can see the dramatic difference between the amounts of salt and fresh water. Instead of using real water cups, turn this activity into a poster to share with your friends.

MATERIALS
• 1 piece of poster board
• green, blue, and black markers
• pencil

1. Draw 100 cups or circles on the poster board with the black marker, making ten rows with ten cups in each row.

2. Color 97 of the cups green. Green represents the world's salt water.

3. Draw ice cubes in two of the cups, using your blue marker.

4. Color the last remaining cup blue. Blue represents the world's fresh water.

These 100 cups represent all the waters of the Earth.
    97% of the Earth's water is salt water.
    2% of the Earth's water is fresh water that is frozen.
    1% of the Earth's water is liquid fresh water.
The entire Earth drinks out of this 1 cup of fresh water. What happens if we pollute this water?

The Water Cycle

As the Sun heats the water of the ocean, **evaporation** takes place. The waters of the Earth are in constant activity. They are always moving, always changing from one state of matter to another. This constant movement and change is called the **water cycle**. It is a closed cycle — not a drop is lost.

A miniature water cycle.

CONDENSATION

PRECIPITATION

EVAPORATION

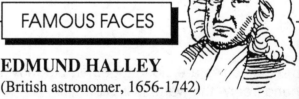

RUN-OFF

Evaporation occurs when water molecules change from liquid to gas because of heating, and rise through the air, mixing with other gases. The warm, moist air rises into the cooler regions of the atmosphere. The rising air cools and begins to **condense**, or change from a gas back to a liquid. The **condensation** takes place around small particles of dust found in the atmosphere. Tiny droplets of water are formed and join together, forming clouds. Depending on the temperature, the water in the clouds returns to the Earth as **precipitation** in the form of rain, snow, sleet, or hail.

FAMOUS FACES

EDMUND HALLEY

(British astronomer, 1656-1742)

Halley, most famous for having a comet named after him, was the first person to realize that water moved over the Earth in a cycle. He said that water evaporated from the Mediterranean Sea into the air and then fell on Europe and northern Africa as rain. The rivers in the region returned large amounts of water to the Mediterranean Sea, and the cycle began again. The real cycle, we've since discovered, is much more complex and variable, but Halley's theory was a simple version of the water cycle that moves water over the entire surface of the Earth.

A Balanced Water Budget

The ocean loses more water through evaporation than it gets back directly in precipitation. The amount of water that runs off land from rainfall and returns to the ocean makes up for this difference. In other words, the water that flows into the ocean from the land, plus the water that falls into the ocean as rain, equals the amount of water that the ocean lost in the beginning through evaporation.

The continents get more precipitation and have less evaporation than the ocean. If you add the amount of water that evaporates from the Earth's land to the amount that runs off into the ocean, it equals the total amount of water the land received. This is called a "water-flow budget," and as you can see, it is very balanced.

ACTION ACTIVITY
MAKE IT RAIN

You can change water vapor from a gaseous state to liquid water by creating your own rainfall.

MATERIALS
- **wide-mouthed jar with a lid**
- **1 cup (250 ml) boiling water**
- **ice cubes**
- **small cloth**
- **adult helper**

1. Stand the jar on the cloth. Ask an adult to pour 1 cup (250 ml) of boiling water into the jar, and seal it. This hot water represents the ocean.

2. Place ice cubes on top of the lid. The ice on the lid represents the colder air high above the water.

3. As the evaporation from the "ocean" reaches the colder air above, condensation forms. Watch closely: After several minutes it will begin to rain over the "ocean."

Are You Drinking George Washington's Bathwater?

The Earth has always had the same amount of water; it just doesn't stay in the same place or in the same state of matter. One drop of water might go from being a part of an iceberg in the Atlantic, to a cloud over a mountain, to rain over a valley, to a tree in a forest, to a teardrop in your eye.

Since the Earth always has the same amount of water, the water that existed in the past continues to stay on Earth and is used over and over as part of the water cycle. A molecule of water from the Nile river during the time of the Pharaohs might be in the food you eat. Water used to raise rice in China might be in the clouds above your head. You could be drinking George Washington's bathwater in your next glass of iced tea.

Properties of Water

What expands as it gets colder, holds more heat than a metal, can carry things heavier than itself, and can move upward against the force of gravity? The answer to this riddle is water! Water is weird, but wonderful. It doesn't act like other matter on Earth. We have already seen that water is different from any other substance, because it can be found in all three states of matter within the natural temperatures of Earth's surface. Water has some other very unusual characteristics, or **properties**.

ACTION ACTIVITIES
PROPERTIES OF WATER

1. Dissolving action: Water is able to dissolve almost anything. It is called the "universal solvent." The water we drink dissolves our food and helps to move it throughout our bodies. Water dissolves the minerals and nutrients in soil and carries them through a plant's roots to its cells. Water helps erode and dissolve many of the rocks on the Earth's surface.

How much can water dissolve? Try this activity to see why water is called the "universal solvent."

MATERIALS

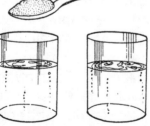

- 2 glasses, each half full of water
- 6 tablespoons of sugar
- 6 tablespoons of salt

1. Fill two glasses with the same amount of water. Put one tablespoon of sugar in one glass and watch as it dissolves.

2. Continue to add sugar, one tablespoon at a time, until you have added 6 tablespoons of sugar. Does the level of water in the glass rise? Compare it to the glass of water without sugar. Water is able to dissolve large amounts of minerals.

3. Add the same amount of salt to the other glass and compare the two.

2. Capillary action: Water molecules have a strong attraction for each other. They will move toward each other, even against the pull of gravity. Water's capillary action helps it move through soil, take nutrients up the stems of plants, and circulate the blood in the bodies of animals.

The capillary action of water is demonstrated in this activity.

MATERIALS

- **water (enough to fill a saucer)**
- **saucer**
- **coffee filter**
- **marker**

1. Cut a coffee filter into a long, narrow strip.

2. Draw a line with a water-based marker 1" (2.5 cm) from one end of the strip.

3. Hold the marked tip of the strip in a saucer of water. The water in the saucer begins to move up the strip because of the capillary action of water. Notice what happens when the water passes through the ink.

3. Surface tension: Water has a high surface tension. **Surface tension** is a force that exists on the surface of liquids where the molecules pull at each other very strongly, forming a kind of "skin." Surface tension is what allows water to make things wet. Water can stick to soil, a table, a washcloth, or an animal's fur. Surface tension is what enables a water bug to walk on the surface of water.

Water's surface tension is so strong that objects such as a sewing needle or a piece of paper can lie on the surface of the water without breaking the surface. This activity demonstrates the strength of surface tension.

MATERIALS
• **glass**
• **water (to completely fill the glass)**
• **15-20 pennies**

1. Place a glass on a flat surface and pour water into the glass until it is completely full.

2. Carefully drop pennies into the water one at a time.

Do this slowly so that the water does not splash. Watch what happens to the water level. The surface molecules will hold tightly, and the water level will rise higher than the edge of the glass.

You can see the properties of water in nature. A water beetle takes advantage of surface tension to walk on water. The beetle is light enough that it does not break the surface "skin." Some types of spiders can also do this.

4. Expanding action: As most matter gets colder, it **contracts**, or shrinks. Not water; it **expands** as it freezes. It is this expansion that makes ice float. Ice is less dense than liquid water. This is why icebergs float on the surface of the ocean instead of sinking to the bottom. Try this activity to prove how water expands when frozen.

MATERIALS
• **clear plastic container**
• **marker or tape**
• **ruler**
• **freezer**

1. Fill the container with water about halfway, and mark the water level on the container with a marker or tape.

2. Place the container in the freezer until the water is frozen.

3. Check the level of the frozen water. It has risen above the original water line, proving that water expands when frozen.

5. Retaining heat: Water can hold large amounts of heat without getting very hot. Boil a pan of water and watch it closely. You will see small bubbles forming along the sides of the pan, and the water will look as if it is ready to boil at any moment. Suddenly, the action seems to stop for a while as if the heat has been turned off, and then it finally erupts into a boil at 212°F (100°C).

What happened during the long wait? The water molecules were absorbing heat from the stove, but not rapidly increasing in temperature. Water molecules can absorb a lot of heat energy. See how much heat water can take before it will boil.

MATERIALS
• **pot**
• **water (enough to fill pot)**
• **candy thermometer (optional)**
• **adult helper**

1. Have an adult boil a pot of water and watch for the effects described above.

2. If you have a candy thermometer, place it in the water and watch what happens to the water temperature during the stages described.

Salt Water

Have you heard the quote "Water, water everywhere and not a drop to drink"? This saying makes sense when you think about trying to drink water from the ocean. Ocean water has the elements found on Earth dissolved within it. The most common elements, sodium (Na) and chlorine (Cl), form the mineral **salt**. Because there is so much salt in ocean water (3.5% of ocean water is salt), only plants and animals that have special ways of removing the salt can use this water in their bodies.

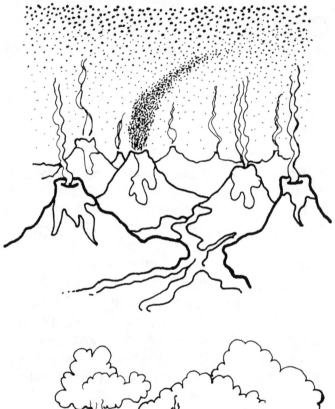

The Formation of the Ocean

No one knows exactly how Earth's ocean was formed, but many scientists think that after the Earth formed, different gases were released from its cooling surface. Hydrogen was one of the gases released. Since hydrogen (H_2) gas is the lightest element, nearly all of this gas floated away into space. However, a very small amount of hydrogen had combined with heavier elements in the crust, such as silicon, carbon, and sulfur. As the planet continued to cool and an atmosphere formed, some of these trapped hydrogen atoms escaped into the atmosphere. When two hydrogen atoms combined with a heavier oxygen atom in the hot atmosphere, water vapor (H_2O) was formed.

As the Earth's surface cooled below the boiling point, water vapor in the air began to condense and fall as rain. It rained for millions of years, filling the ocean and every other hollow place on the surface of the Earth. This early ocean was composed of fresh rainwater, with a few elements mixed in from the surface crust.

Two of these elements, chlorine and sodium, when combined in the form of sodium chloride (common salt), give ocean water its salty taste. Other elements found in seawater, although in much smaller quantities, are magnesium, sulfur, calcium, and potassium.

Protecting the Ocean

Even though geographers have given names to the regions of ocean outlined by the land, it is important to view the oceans as one world ocean. Things that happen in one part of the ocean affect life in other areas of the ocean.

Farming for krill (small shrimplike organisms) in the Pacific will affect the food chain of the entire ocean. Krill is food for small fish and whales. Giant oil spills in the Persian Gulf and Alaska's Prince William Sound will cause damage to thousands of plants and animals, changing the balance of the entire ocean. Excessive fishing in the Atlantic Ocean might cause the extinction of other animals dependent upon the fish that are taken. All nations must work together to protect and preserve the world's ocean.

ACTION ACTIVITY
SALT IN AND OUT OF WATER

Discover what happens to the salt in water when the water evaporates.

MATERIALS
- ¼ cup (62.5 ml) table salt
- pitcher
- 6 cups (1.4 liters) warm water
- a flat pan
- a sunny spot indoors or outdoors

1. Mix ¼ cup (62.5 ml) of salt and 6 cups (1.4 liters) of water in the pitcher. Allow all of the salt to dissolve in the water. This mixture is 4% salt to 96% water, about the same as the amount of salt in the ocean. (The composition of seawater is almost the same all over the world because of the mixing action of waves and currents.)

2. Pour the salt water into the flat pan and place it in a sunny location. Allow it to stay in this location for several days.

3. Notice that the water level gets lower each day as the water slowly evaporates. When all of the water has evaporated, there will be a layer of salt in the bottom of the pan and along the sides.

4. Carefully remove all of the salt from the pan and measure it. Was any of the salt removed through evaporation?

Fresh Water

Nature does not distribute fresh water evenly. Some regions of the Earth receive over 400 inches (1000 cm) of rain each year, while other regions might not receive any rain for several years. If we could collect all of the fresh water on Earth and divide it equally among the regions of the Earth, and use the water wisely, there would be fresh water for all people, animals, crops, and industrial needs.

Uses of Fresh Water

As the world's population increases, the demand for fresh water increases. Fresh water is used for drinking, cooking, and bathing, as well as washing cars, clothes, and dishes. It is pumped into desert regions for irrigation, it is used to maintain golf courses and fill swimming pools, and it is used in many kinds of manufacturing. Fresh water is even used to flush toilets and disperse industrial waste.

FIND IT

Water has always been a factor in the development of civilization. Early civilizations developed along various rivers around the world. Find these areas of ancient civilization on the map. Then look at a world atlas to see where the current population has settled.

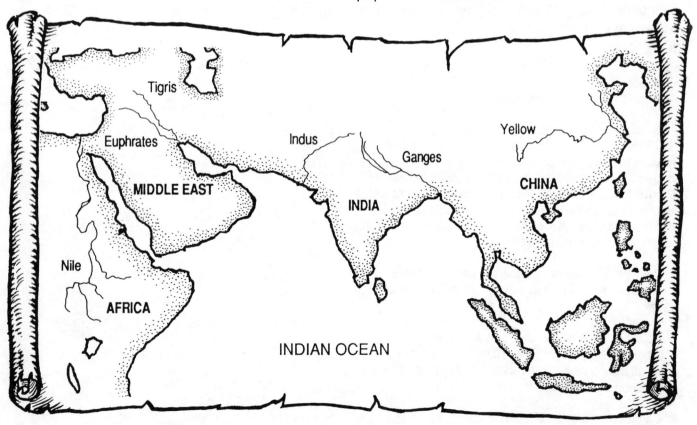

Compared to the amount of salt water on the Earth, there is very little fresh water. All land plants and animals must have fresh water to live.

Throughout history, mankind has searched for ways to convert salt water into fresh water.

ACTION ACTIVITY
PURE, FRESH WATER

Salt water is not fit for humans to drink. This activity illustrates one method of purifying water that is salty or polluted (though not all pollutants can be removed this easily).

MATERIALS
- vegetable food coloring
- potting soil
- 4 tablespoons (60 ml) salt
- 2 cups (500 ml) water
- a pan
- hot plate or stove top
- aluminum foil
- a bowl
- adult helper

1. Have an adult place the water in the pan and allow it to heat slowly to near boiling. Add the salt, several drops of food coloring, and a small amount of potting soil to the water. This water is not good for drinking; it is not pure.

2. Make a tent out of the foil as illustrated. Place the foil over the pan of water and allow one end of the foil to extend over the bowl as illustrated.

3. Have an adult turn up the heat and bring the water to a boil. As the water vapor formed by the boiling water reaches the foil, it condenses and water is formed. This water will slowly move along the foil into the bowl.

4. Observe the water in the bowl. Does it have any color? Does it look like the water in the pan? When it cools, dip your finger in and taste a drop. Is it salty? What has happened?

Fresh Water Underground

If you have ever gone for a walk in the rain, or if you go outside right after a rain, you will see several different things happening to the fresh water that has fallen. As rain falls on the ground around you, some of it soaks into the ground and waters plants, while some of it goes deep into the rocks below the surface soil. Some of the rain moves over the ground on its way to join other water in streams, lakes, and rivers. Some of it evaporates because of wind or heat from the Sun.

Ground Water

Although it is hard to believe, there is more fresh water under the ground than above. All the lakes, rivers, springs, marshes, and swamps in the world hold only 2.5% of the water found underground. This water is held by the rocks of the crust. It flows through cracks and crevices in the crust or collects in hollow spaces between rocks.

Some rocks are very **porous**. This means that they have lots of little air spaces that can hold water, like a sponge. Porous rocks, like sandstone and limestone, are able to hold large amounts of water.

Some rocks have very low **porosity**. Igneous rocks like granite do not hold water; however, granite will allow water to flow through its cracks and breaks.

A rock that allows water to pass through it is called **permeable**. Ground water will continue to be pulled downward by gravity until it reaches rock that is **impermeable**, or rock that will not allow the water to pass through.

When the permeable rock above the impermeable rock layer becomes **saturated**, or full of water, the water must find other places to go. A **water table** is the highest level of ground water in the saturated rock.

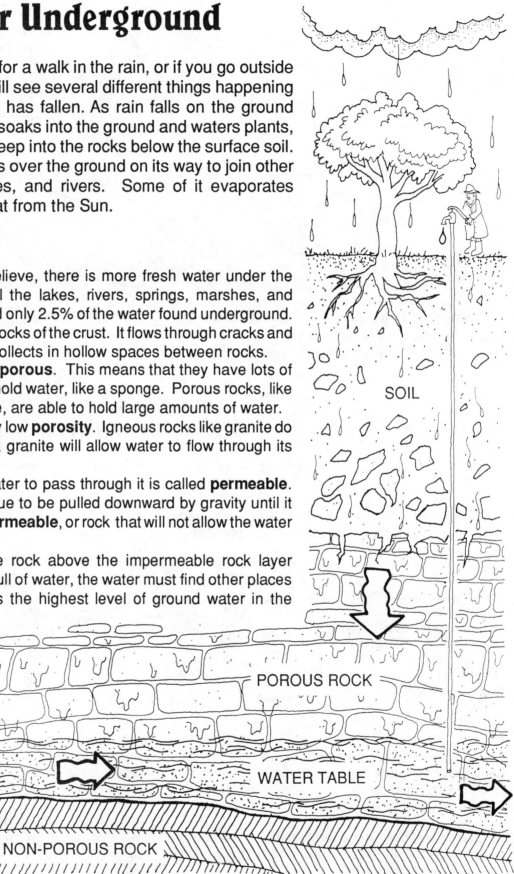

SOIL

POROUS ROCK

WATER TABLE

NON-POROUS ROCK

🌂 You may have heard people talk about water as being either hard or soft. **Hard water** is water that contains dissolved minerals, such as calcium and magnesium compounds. Because it is difficult to get water with dissolved minerals in it to form a lather, it is called "hard water." Water "softeners" remove minerals from the water.

🌂 Ground water is the source of 55% of the water used in the United States.

ACTION ACTIVITY
DILUTION IS NOT THE SOLUTION TO POLLUTION

Will adding fresh water to polluted water purify it, or will you just have more polluted water?

MATERIALS
- **4 clear plastic cups, glasses, or jars, all the same size**
- **red food coloring**
- **water**
- **pitcher**
- **measuring cup**

1. Pour 1 cup (250 ml) of water into one of the glasses. Add 2 or 3 drops of food coloring. This water is now "polluted" by "chemicals" that have moved into the water table. This is glass #1.

2. Pour ½ cup (125 ml) of polluted water from glass #1 into another cup, #2. Also add ½ cup (125 ml) of fresh water to cup #2. Fresh water has been added to the water table.

3. Pour ½ cup (125 ml) of water from cup #2 into another cup, #3. Add ½ cup (125 ml) of fresh water to cup #3. What is happening to the "chemicals" in the "ground water"?

4. Pour ½ cup (125 ml) of water from cup #3 into another cup, #4. Add ½ cup (125 ml) of fresh water to cup #4. Now what has happened to the "chemicals"? Have they gone away?

When chemicals, oil, fertilizers, or any other substances get into our water supply, they do not go away when more water is added. Instead, they spread through the added water, and continue to pollute. Dilution is not the solution to pollution.

Surface Water

Have you ever driven over a bridge that crossed a large river? As you look down at the river, you can get an idea of its size and strength. The water is strong and fast-moving, and often you can see that it carries huge logs and rocks. The waters of rivers cut and shape the surface of the land.

The Growth of a River

The surface water that becomes runoff water after a rain, the spring water that seeps out of the side of a hill, or the water from the melting of a glacier can all give birth to a stream that might someday become a river. These small streams are fed by runoff water. Most of the giant rivers of the world began their lives as small mountain streams.

The point where a river begins is called its **source**. The path the river takes over the land is called its **course**. The point where the river finally reaches sea level and becomes part of the world's ocean is the **mouth** of the river.

Small streams cause **erosion**. They break up rock and wash away soil around them. Since many of them begin in mountains or hills, their water moves quickly downward, cutting deeper and deeper paths into the surface of the land. The most erosion occurs in the upper course of a river or stream where the water moves with the most force.

The stream carries the eroded material, or **sediment**, to new areas. More and more water is pulled into this waterway from surrounding drainage and runoff. Smaller streams become part of this growing stream and add their own eroded material and water sources.

The water slows as it gets closer to sea level. Much of the eroded material in the water begins to settle out. Deposits of sediment can be found at the point where this fresh water meets a standing body of water — for example, a freshwater lake or the salt-water ocean.

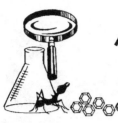

ACTION ACTIVITY
SUGAR CUBE CANYON

The Grand Canyon is an example of how water carves the Earth. This activity will illustrate the same type of carving action.

MATERIALS
- **a box of sugar cubes**
- **water**
- **large nail**
- **adult helper**

1. Have an adult helper cut off one side of a box of sugar cubes.

2. Have the adult helper punch holes in one end of the box.

3. Place the box of sugar cubes on a slight angle, with the open side up and the "holey" end at the lowest point.

4. Watch what happens to the sugar cubes as the water slowly "erodes" them. Compare this sugar cube canyon to the Grand Canyon.

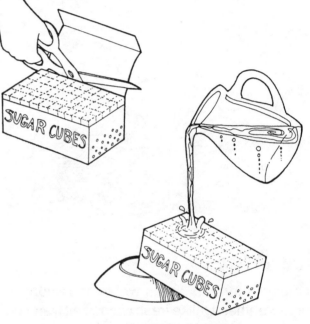

Frozen Water

Polar bears are often seen floating on sheets of ice in the Arctic Ocean. Some spend their entire lives without ever setting foot on land. These giant bears are able to live like this because the waters of the frigid polar regions have ice all year long.

Fresh Water

A large amount of the Earth's fresh water is trapped in ice. Nearly two-thirds of all the fresh water on Earth is frozen in icebergs and ice packs in the sea, and in icecaps and glaciers on land. Ice packs are formed from frozen salt water. Icebergs, icecaps, and glaciers form on land and are made completely of fresh water.

Ice Packs

Ice packs form in ocean waters in regions with frigid weather. Unlike fresh water, salt water does not freeze at 32°F (0°C). The large amount of dissolved salts in seawater lowers the freezing point to 28.6°F (-1.9°C).

As freezing winds blow over the water surface, small ice crystals begin to form. These ice crystals are made of pure fresh water. The salt molecules are trapped in liquid around these ice crystals. As these ice crystals collect together, plates of ice are formed that thicken with time.

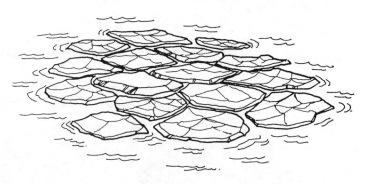

Icecaps

About 6 million square miles (9.6 million square km) of the Earth's surface is covered by icecaps. Giant sheets of ice up to 6,000 feet (1800 m) deep cover Antarctica and Greenland. Smaller ice sheets lie over Iceland, parts of Scandinavia, and the Canadian Islands. Sometimes entire mountains can be completely covered.

Icebergs

When glaciers reach the ocean and break off into the water, an **iceberg** is formed. Since icebergs form as ice on land, they are made purely of fresh water, like giant ice cubes.

Icebergs that form in the Arctic move south along the eastern coast of Canada to Newfoundland. Icebergs that form in the Antarctic have been seen as far north as the south island of New Zealand at 40° south latitude.

A Famous Iceberg

In 1912, the Titanic, the largest ship in the world, was thought to be strong enough to withstand a collision with an iceberg. On the night of April 14, 1912, on its first voyage, the Titantic sank after hitting a small iceberg in the North Atlantic. About 1,500 of the 2,200 passengers were lost. Today, the International Ice Patrol keeps track of the icebergs in the North American shipping lanes.

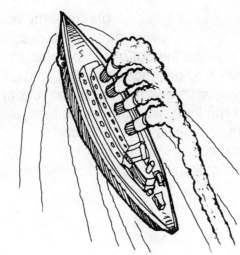

ACTION ACTIVITY
ICE-COLD

Freezing is the process that turns a liquid into a solid when its temperature is reduced to a certain point. For example, water freezes at 32°F (0°C). You can watch the temperature change as frozen solid matter (ice) is placed in liquid water.

MATERIALS
- **glass of water**
- **ice cubes**
- **thermometer**

1. Fill a glass with water. Place the thermometer in the glass. Read the temperature.

2. Add ice to the water. Watch what happens to the temperature of the water.

3. Ice is a solid, and it needs heat energy to melt. The heat energy needed to melt the ice comes from the water surrounding the ice cubes. As the heat energy leaves the water and melts the ice, the water is cooled.

4. Can you make this cooling process go faster? Do this same activity again, except this time, shake the ice around in the glass every 30 seconds and then measure the temperature of the water. How does this shaking make a difference? Why?

Glaciers

A melting glacier in Italy, near the Austrian border, deposited something very unusual in September 1991—the preserved body of a 5,000-year-old man. Scientists are not sure why the man died while at a campsite away from his home. Some of the objects found with the body include a bronze axe, a stone knife, and a wooden backpack. Look at the illustration below to see how this 5,000-year-old glacier grave was formed.

Ice That Moves on Land

Year after year, snow collects in the high mountain valleys and snowfields between mountain peaks. The weight of the layers of snow compresses the deepest snow into ice. Year after year, as new snow falls, the ice becomes thicker and denser, and a glacier is formed. Due to its own weight and the slope of the mountain, the glacier moves very slowly down the mountainside. Year after year, the glacier continues to grow and move.

As glaciers move, rocks and sediment are picked up in the ice at the bottom of the glacier. This debris is carried long distances over the land. These rocks and sediments scratch and tear at the soil under the glacier as it moves over the land, wearing the soil smooth, much like sandpaper smoothing a piece of rough wood.

As the tip of a glacier reaches warmer, lower land, it begins to melt. The debris carried by the glacier is deposited on the land at the end of the glacier's journey.

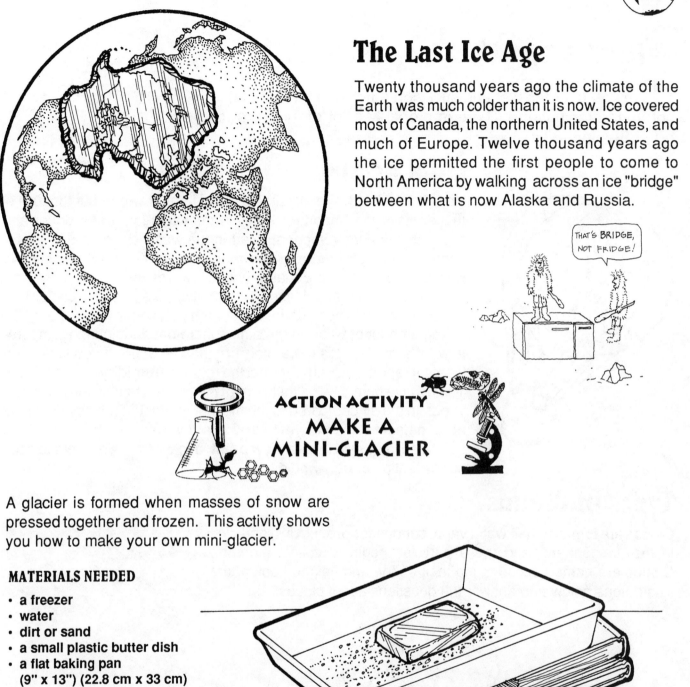

The Last Ice Age

Twenty thousand years ago the climate of the Earth was much colder than it is now. Ice covered most of Canada, the northern United States, and much of Europe. Twelve thousand years ago the ice permitted the first people to come to North America by walking across an ice "bridge" between what is now Alaska and Russia.

THAT'S BRIDGE, NOT FRIDGE!

ACTION ACTIVITY
MAKE A MINI-GLACIER

A glacier is formed when masses of snow are pressed together and frozen. This activity shows you how to make your own mini-glacier.

MATERIALS NEEDED

- a freezer
- water
- dirt or sand
- a small plastic butter dish
- a flat baking pan
  (9" x 13") (22.8 cm x 33 cm)

1. Fill the butter dish with water and place it in a freezer until it is frozen solid.

2. Cover the bottom of the flat baking pan with dirt or sand. Place the pan at an angle as illustrated, forming a "mountain slope."

3. Remove the frozen "glacier" from the dish. Place the "glacier" at the top of the "mountain."

4. Watch the "glacier" as it slowly moves down the "mountain." What happens to the "land" beneath it? Does the "glacier" collect dirt as it moves? What would happen if the "mountain slope" were steeper? Try it and find out.

Water Vapor

Have you ever felt wet and sticky on a hot summer day? It is not your imagination. There is probably a lot of moisture, or **humidity**, in the air.

Light as Air

Very little of Earth's total water is in the form of vapor, but the .001% that exists is very important to life. Water vapor forms into clouds and rain. It plays a very important part in the water cycle (p. 58). Water vapor also helps to control the temperature of Earth's climate. As warm, moist air at the Equator moves towards the poles (p. 82), the water vapor in the air releases its heat along the way as it cools. This keeps the colder areas of the Earth from getting too cold.

The amount of water in the atmosphere depends on the temperature. Warm air holds more moisture than cold air. If you listen to a weather report, you will hear what the **relative humidity** is in your area. The relative humidity is a measure of the amount of moisture, or water vapor, in the air compared to the maximum amount the air could hold at its present temperature. Air with a relative humidity of 100% is saturated, also said to be at **dew point**, because if the air were to cool, condensation or dew would form.

Types of Clouds

Clouds are formed when water vapor condenses around dust particles in the atmosphere, and these particles begin to collect together. Clouds are named according to their shape and height. Look at the illustrations below and answer the questions about clouds.

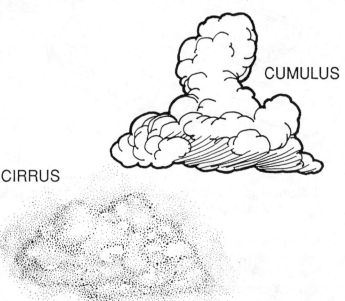

CUMULUS

STRATUS

CIRRUS

FIND IT

Find the clouds that look like cotton balls. What are they called?
What are the highest, thinnest clouds called?
Which cloud is most concentrated and looks like it could produce a thunderstorm?

ACTION ACTIVITY
MAKE A CLOUD

You can make a small "cloud" in the kitchen, using common materials, by following these simple steps with an adult helper.

MATERIALS
- **1-gallon, restaurant-size glass jar** (Check with the school cafeteria or a restaurant to see if they might give you one. Make sure it does not have any cracks and that you can easily put your fist into the opening.)
- **timer/clock**
- **marker**
- **ruler**
- **extra-large rubber balloon**
- **scissors**
- **book**
- **teaspoon of chalk dust**
- **water**
- **large rubber band**
- **safety glasses**
- **adult helper**

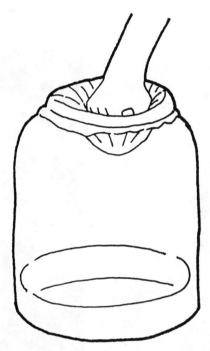

1. Pour water into the jar so that at least 1" (2.54 cm) covers the bottom.

2. Cut the neck off the balloon as illustrated. Stretch the balloon over the top of the jar and put the book on top of the balloon to hold it in place.

3. Let the jar sit for 10 minutes.

4. Put on safety glasses (to protect your eyes from the chalk dust). Lift up a small section of the balloon and quickly add chalk dust. Put the balloon back in place and secure it with a rubber band around the rim of the jar.

5. Push your fist against the balloon until your fist is inside the jar. Hold for 10 seconds (approximate time by counting 1001, 1002, 1003, etc.), then remove your hand quickly. This action will suddenly cool the air in the jar and cause it to condense around the particles. As a result, a cloud forms inside the jar.

Chapter 5

The Atmosphere

Take a deep breath. You are breathing in gases that are needed by all animals and plants on the Earth. This would not have been possible 4.5 billion years ago because the Earth's atmosphere was very different. Earth probably looked like one of the gaseous outer planets (Jupiter, Uranus, Neptune) in our Solar System at that time. Gases formed a thick atmosphere above a dense core. As time passed and the Earth continued to condense, forming the mantle and the crust, many of these gases burned off into space.

The molten crust and volcanic activity released other gases such as nitrogen, ammonia, carbon dioxide, water vapor, and tiny amounts of oxygen. The Earth's early atmosphere was poisonous.

Over millions of years, the atmosphere began to change. In this chapter we will look at the results of these changes: the development of an atmosphere that supports life.

Composition of Earth's Atmosphere

Oxygen has been called the most important element on Earth. This is because so many things—living and nonliving— depend on oxygen. Many rocks that make up the Earth's surface were formed when oxygen was combined with other common elements. Without oxygen, fires could not burn, plants and animals could not live, and there would be no water or clouds.

Oxygen for Life

Where did oxygen come from? It was not present in Earth's early atmosphere. As the surface of the Earth cooled, water vapor in the atmosphere condensed and fell to Earth as rain, forming the world's ocean. The first plants, probably tiny algae (some of the simplest plants known), began to grow and develop at depths beyond the reach of the Sun's harmful ultraviolet radiation. These plants produced their own food by a process called **photosynthesis.** (See pages 90 to 91.) During photosynthesis, plants release oxygen molecules (O_2) into the atmosphere.

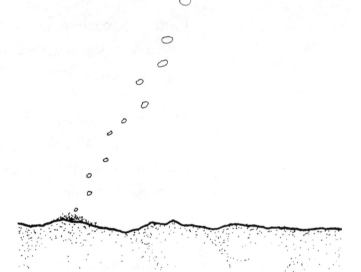

The Ozone Layer

In the air, the molecules of oxygen (O_2) were broken down by radiation into single atoms of oxygen (O), called **free oxygen**. Some of the single oxygen atoms joined with oxygen molecules to form **ozone** (O_3) gas. Ozone is very important to the Earth's atmosphere. Ozone absorbs most of the Sun's harmful ultraviolet radiation.

Until the ozone layer was formed, nothing could live on land. About 420 million years ago, the protective ozone layer was complete, and plants first began to grow on land. Again, because of photosynthesis, these plants produced more oxygen, and Earth began to develop an atmosphere safe for land animals.

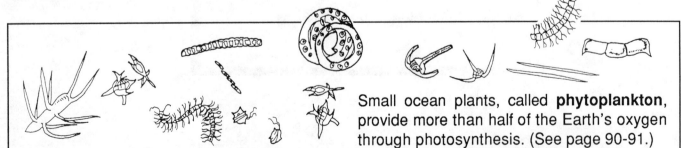

Small ocean plants, called **phytoplankton**, provide more than half of the Earth's oxygen through photosynthesis. (See page 90-91.)

FIND IT

The list to the right shows the gases currently found in Earth's atmosphere. Find these elements in the Periodic Table of Elements (p. 25). Look at their **atomic number,** which indicates their weight. Which gases are the heaviest? The lightest?

Oxygen is heavier than nitrogen, and it is concentrated in the lowest levels of the atmosphere. Earth's atmosphere also contains water vapor, dust, smoke, salt, man-made pollution, and some volcanic ash.

- nitrogen, N_2— 78%

- oxygen, O_2— 21%

- argon, Ar— 0.9%

- carbon dioxide, CO_2 (which is photosynthesized by plants)— .03%

- some neon, helium, ozone, and hydrogen, with minute traces of krypton, methane, xenon, and other gases

ACTION ACTIVITY
AIR IS EVERYWHERE

To demonstrate that air is everywhere, try this activity.

MATERIALS
- a clear glass
- a paper towel
- a bucket of water

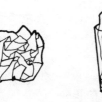

1. Wad up a paper towel and push it into the bottom of a glass so it will not fall out.

2. Turn the glass upside down and quickly push the glass straight down to the bottom of the bucket of water. Allow the glass to touch the bottom as you hold it in place.

3. Pull the glass straight out of the water. Do not tilt the glass. Remove the paper towel. Is it wet?

    The paper towel is dry because the glass was filled with air when it was placed in the water. Air is everywhere. It is

matter and it does take up space. In this case, the air filled the glass and prevented the water from touching the paper towel.

4. Repeat the experiment. This time, before lifting the glass out of the bucket, tilt the glass to the side. The large bubble that escapes to the top of the bucket is the air that was inside the glass. Take the glass out of the water and discover what has happened to the paper towel since the air was removed.

Layer after Layer of Atmosphere

Air was once thought of as a shell that surrounded the Earth's land and water. The early Greeks believed that above this shell of air was a shell of fire. Lightning was their "proof" of this outer ring of fire.

exosphere

Today we know that the Earth's atmosphere is a thin layer of gases, dust particles, and water vapor. The atmosphere protects life on Earth from the deadly ultraviolet rays found in sunlight, it traps the Sun's heat and acts as a "blanket" through the night, and it provides a place for weather to happen.

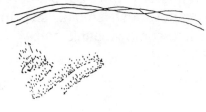

The Earth's atmosphere can be divided into four layers. Each layer has a different density, temperature, and composition of gases. These layers of air are called the **troposphere, stratosphere, ionosphere,** and **exosphere.**

Exosphere

The **exosphere** begins 300 miles (480 km) above the surface of the Earth. This part of the atmosphere has the fewest gases. Atoms of hydrogen, oxygen, and helium can be found here.

ionosphere

Ionosphere

The **ionosphere** is found above the stratosphere, from 30 to 300 miles (48 to 480 km) high. This layer can be divided into two sections with different temperatures: the **mesosphere** and the **thermosphere.** The ionosphere is where the aurora borealis and the aurora australis occur. These displays of natural light glow and flicker at night during certain times of the year. The aurora borealis occurs in the sky of the Northern Hemisphere; the aurora australis can be seen in the Southern Hemisphere.

Stratosphere

stratosphere

The **stratosphere**, starting at 6 miles (9.7 km) above the poles and 10 miles (16.1 km) above the equator, is a dry layer of air above the troposphere that reaches a height of 30 miles (48 km). This is where the ozone gas "shield" is found. It protects us by absorbing and reflecting much of the ultraviolet radiation from space away from the Earth's surface.

Troposphere

troposphere

Over 50% of the air in the Earth's atmosphere can be found within 3 miles (5 km) of the Earth's surface. Seventy-five percent can be found in the first 6 miles (9.7 km) of the atmosphere above the poles and the first 10 miles (16.1 km) of the atmosphere above the Equator. This region is called the **troposphere.** The main gases in this layer are nitrogen and oxygen. It is within the troposphere that we find weather.

Earth

What Is Air Pressure?

All matter takes up space and has mass, or weight, including gases. If something has weight, it presses against other objects. All of the air in the atmosphere presses down against the Earth's surface. This is called air pressure.

The higher you go in the Earth's atmosphere, the less air pressure there is. This is because there are fewer and fewer molecules of gas in the atmosphere at these levels, and the molecules that are present are spaced very far apart. Less air, or fewer gases, means less pressure on objects in these regions.

Less air also means humans will have more difficulty in breathing. For example, when people who live at sea level climb a mountain for the first time, they will have some difficulty breathing. Mountain air is said to be "thin." Airplanes that fly in the stratosphere have to have special cabins that provide the same pressurized mixture of air that passengers breathe on the land.

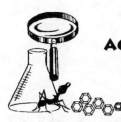

ACTION ACTIVITY
PUSH UP

MATERIALS
• **glass of water or soft drink**
• **a straw**

AIR PRESSURE

1. Place the straw in the glass of liquid.

2. Gently suck on the straw, and you will remove the air in the straw.

3. When you remove the air from the straw, the air pressure on the surface of the liquid in the glass becomes greater than the air pressure in the straw, and the liquid is pushed up the straw.

Weather

People love to talk about the weather. They often describe it as being good or bad. Whether weather is good or bad depends on what people want or need. Weather is worth talking about. It is very important to Earth. What is weather? Weather is what happens in the atmosphere at a particular place and time. Weather is temperature, precipitation, wind speed, and humidity. The Earth's weather is a result of the Sun's effect on the Earth's land and water surface.

Convection

Since the Earth is round, the Sun heats the Earth's surface unequally. The Equator receives the most heat and the polar regions the least. The air heated at the Equator rises and moves in currents going north and currents going south toward the Earth's poles. This movement is called **convection**. A **convection cell** is an area of air moving in a great circle. A convection cell is illustrated in the room pictured. When the air is heated it rises from the surface into the atmosphere, cools, and falls back to the surface, where it is re-heated and rises, and the current begins again.

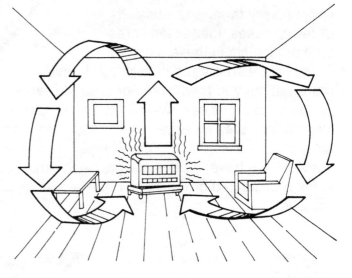

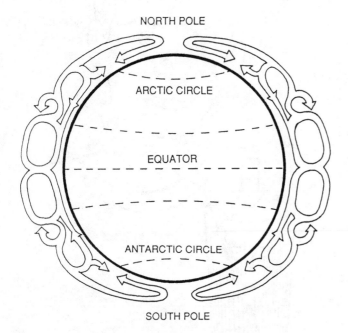

If the Earth's surface were smooth, and the Earth did not rotate on its axis, there would be only two convection cells—from the Equator north and south to the poles and back to the Equator.

However, the Earth has mountains that can affect the flow of the air, and the Earth does rotate on its axis. Some of the rising air from the Equator cools and sinks at different latitudes on its way to the Earth's poles. Only part of the air that began at the Equator finally reaches the polar regions, and here it begins to flow back toward the Equator.

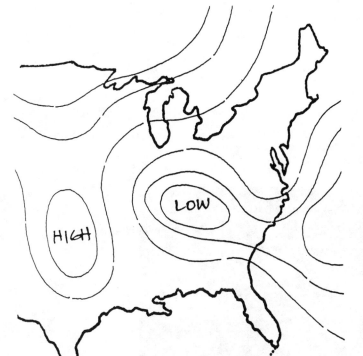

Wind

This up-and-down movement of air in the Earth's lower atmosphere results in areas of high pressure and low pressure. The differences in temperature and air pressure on the Earth's surface cause the air in the Earth's lower atmosphere to move, and the result of this movement is **wind.**

Air that is heated by the Sun expands, becomes lighter, and rises. This happens in a low pressure area. As it rises, cool air moves in to take its place near the surface of the Earth. This produces wind. Wind also results from air moving toward areas of low pressure and away from areas of high pressure. Find the high and low pressure areas on the weather map.

ACTION ACTIVITY
RAIN GAUGE

To measure the amount of rainfall in a certain period, we collect the rain in a rain gauge.

MATERIALS
- **wide-mouthed jar (peanut butter jars work well)**
- **black permanent marker**
- **small, tall jar (small olive jar works well)**
- **12-inch (30.5-cm) ruler**

1. Use the permanent marker to indicate inches (or centimeters) on the wide-mouthed jar. Keep this rain gauge in a safe place outside. Make sure it will not collect water that could splash up from the surface on which it is placed. It is best to place a rain gauge on a stand, such as an upside-down flower pot.

Use this rain gauge to collect and measure rainfall during heavy rains. You will also need the small rain gauge (see below) for measuring small amounts of rainfall. It's important that the openings to the jar are the same width as the rest of the jar so that you capture all the rain for that area.

2. Fill your rain gauge with 1 inch (2.5 cm) of water. Pour this water into the small, tall jar.

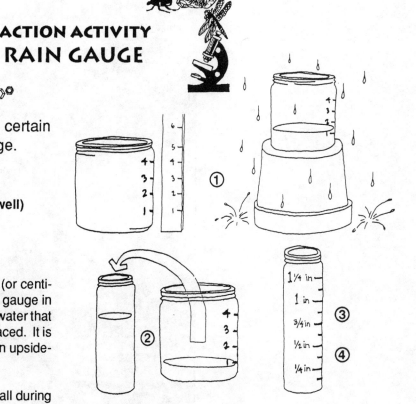

3. Draw a line at the top of the water line and label it "1 inch" or "2.5 cm."

4. Divide the space below this mark in halves (1.3 cm), fourths (0.6 cm), and eighths (0.3 cm). It is much easier to see ⅛ inch of rain in this container than in the wide container you used to collect the rain.

Chapter 6

Life on Earth

Your body has something in common with all of the things we have examined in this book: the land, the water, and the air. Can you guess what this might be? Every part of you is made of the same elements that compose the nonliving parts of the Earth. The most common elements in your body are carbon (C), hydrogen (H), oxygen (O), nitrogen (N), sulfur (S), phosphorus (P), potassium (K), calcium (Ca), iron (Fe), and magnesium (Mg).

We have seen these same elements in other places. Hydrogen and oxygen form water. Nitrogen is the most common element in the air. Nitrogen, phosphorus, and potassium are found naturally in the soil; they can be bought as fertilizers to help plants grow. Iron and magnesium form the inner and outer core of the Earth; they are found in small amounts in the Earth's crust and seawater. These are the elements that are most common to life, yet these same elements compose nonliving matter. What makes living matter different? Let's investigate life on Earth.

What Is Life?

It is not easy to define life, or even to state the meaning of life. Scientists, philosophers, poets, and teenagers have been trying to do this since ancient times. It is easier to talk about things that are part of life.

Living Things

Living things grow, and most living things can move. Living things consume food and water, using them to produce energy. They reproduce other, similar living organisms. They react to outside factors such as heat, light, or pressure.

Many nonliving things have some of these characteristics. For example, a rock can move, but it cannot move on its own. It moves because of gravity. But to be considered a living thing, an organism must have all, not just some, of these characteristics.

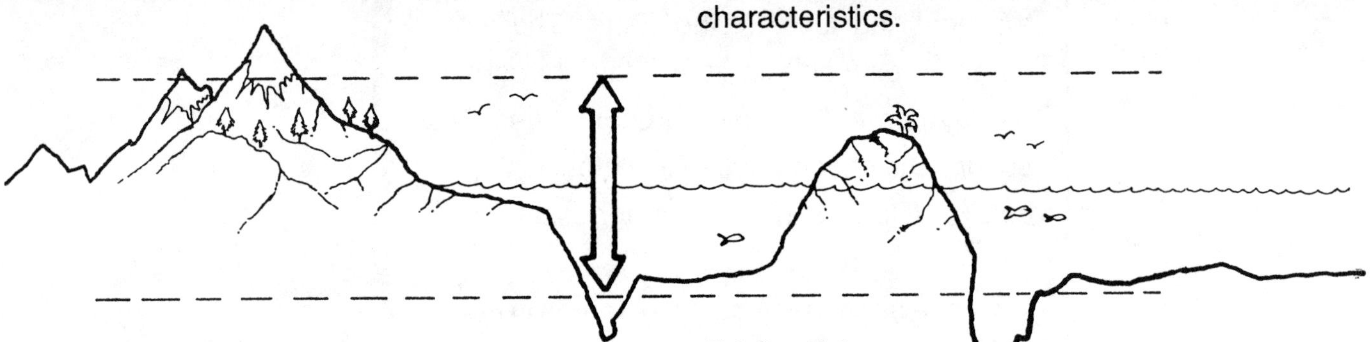

Life Line

Compared to the thickness of the Earth, life is found in a very thin section of the surface, where all the ingredients necessary for life (temperature, gases to breathe, food and water) exist.

This "zone of life" is from 27,000 feet (8,100 meters) above sea level to 23,000 feet (6,900 meters) below sea level. Living things are not found above or below these "life lines."

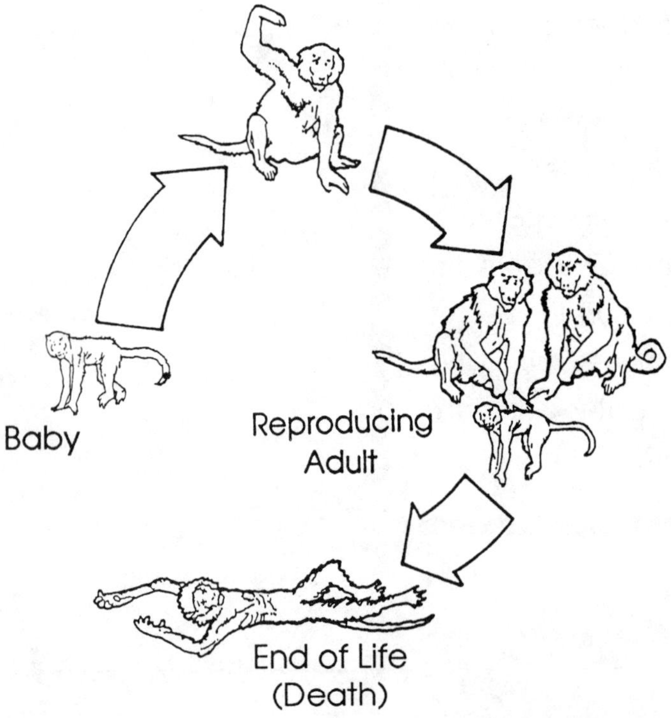

Life Cycles

It is exciting to see new life beginning. Small green sprouts from grass seeds, microscopic spiders, tiny scared lizards, noisy hatchlings in a nest, and a sleeping baby in a stroller are examples of new life. All these various life forms will pass through the same basic cycle of life illustrated here. They will live, and they will die. Death is an important part of this cycle because it makes room for new life.

Baby

Reproducing
Adult

End of Life
(Death)

Three Kinds of Living Organisms

All living organisms can be divided into three main groups: organisms that produce their own food; organisms that cannot produce their own food, so they eat other organisms; and organisms that break down other organisms that have died.

Plants are organisms that produce their own food. They are called **producers**.

Animals are organisms that cannot produce their own food. They must eat, or consume, other organisms. They are called **consumers**.

Bacteria and fungi are organisms that break down organisms that have died. They are called **decomposers**.

 **FIND IT**

Identify the organisms below as either producers, consumers, or decomposers.

Plants

Plants are called producers because they produce their own food from water, nutrients, and sunlight, and because they are responsible ultimately for all food eaten by other organisms. For example, let's look at something that the average human animal in the United States eats close to 200 of in a year's time—a hamburger—and see how it is a product of plants.

Have a Plantburger!

The next time you eat a hamburger, think about all the plants that helped to produce it.

- Wheat is ground into flour to make the hamburger bun.

- The lettuce, sliced tomatoes, and chopped onions are freshly grown.

- Pickles are vegetables that have been in vinegar and spices.

- Mustard is made from the ground-up seeds of the mustard plant.

- Catsup is made from tomatoes.

- The beef comes from cattle, an animal (a consumer) that eats plants—grains, hay, and grass.

Balance of Life

Plants are found almost anywhere on Earth. Over 350,000 different kinds of plants exist that have been identified, and there are probably thousands that haven't even been seen or studied. Most animals eat plants, but some animals eat other animals that eat plants.

For there to be a balance of life on Earth, there have to be a lot more plants than animals, and a lot more animals that eat plants than animals that eat meat. Plants are the first link in the chain of food production that supports life on Earth.

ACTION ACTIVITY
MAKING A PLANT PRESS

Collecting and pressing leaves, flowers, and seeds is easy when you make your own press. Be careful not to collect leaves from poisonous plants such as poison ivy. Remember: "Leaves of three, let it be."

MATERIALS
- newspaper
- paper towels
- 2 pieces of heavy cardboard
- 4 large, strong rubber bands or
  4 pieces of heavy cord or string
- hammer and a nail
- an old board
- pencil and small notebook
- 2-inch (5-cm) tape, clear or colored
- adult helper

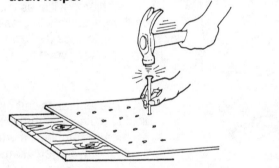

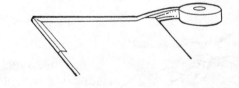

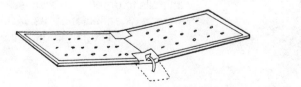

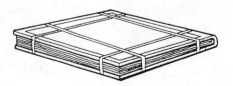

1. To make the plant press, cut 2 pieces of cardboard half the size of a page of your local newspaper. Heavy cardboard may be difficult to find. Get help from an adult if you need to cut up a box.

2. Place the cardboard on top of the wood and have an adult tap the nail through the cardboard, forming rows of holes. You can take an object that fits through the holes and press it around the edges to make the holes larger.

3. Cover the edges of the cardboard with the tape. Place four strips of tape around each board, as illustrated. You might find it easier to keep your plants and papers from slipping out of your plant press if you hinge it together with wide tape on one side.

4. Cut large amounts of newspaper into half sheets. Place this newspaper between the cardboard. Between every 8 to 10 sheets of paper, insert one paper towel.

5. When finished, place the rubber bands around the boards, or use string or ribbon ties.

6. After you have collected your leaves, flowers, and seeds, place them as soon as possible in your press. Close the press, tie it shut, lay it down on a hard surface, and place a heavy object (books, bricks, etc.) on top of it.

7. Leave your specimens in the press for a couple of weeks until they have completely dried out. After one week, check them every few days and feel if they are dry. When they are dry, they should have retained their color and smell (especially flowers). Be careful when handling the dried specimens, as they are fragile and can break easily.

8. You can make wall decorations by pasting your specimens to a sheet of colored paper or poster board and framing it. You can also decorate a small box by pasting the specimens to the top or sides and having an adult varnish the entire box.

Photosynthesis

When you get tired and hungry, do you feel weak? What do you need to help you get some energy—a sunny day or a sandwich? If you eat something, your energy will usually return. This is true for most animals.

If you were a green plant, you would rather have a sunny day to get energy. Plants get their energy directly from the Sun. With this energy they make their own food.

Green plants produce their own food through a process called **photosynthesis** (foto-**sin**-tha-sis), which means "making things with light." That is exactly what plants do with the sunlight they absorb: they make food, called **glucose**, a sugar.

How Photosynthesis Works

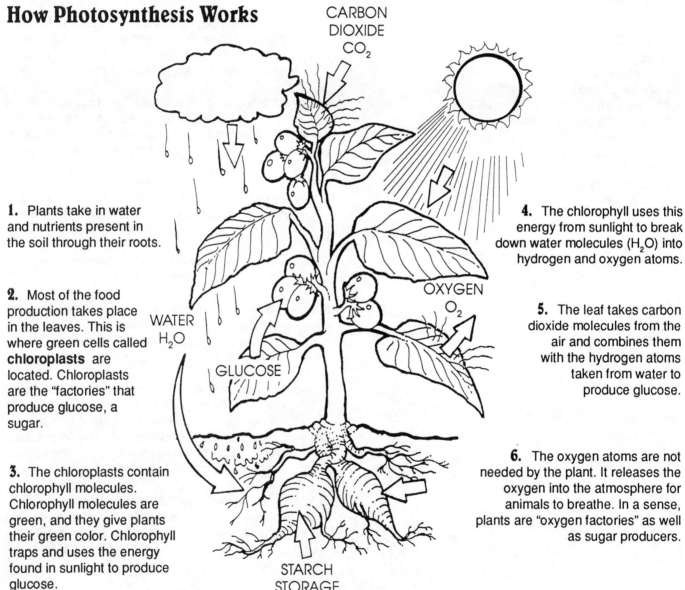

CARBON DIOXIDE CO$_2$

OXYGEN O$_2$

WATER H$_2$O

GLUCOSE

STARCH STORAGE

1. Plants take in water and nutrients present in the soil through their roots.

2. Most of the food production takes place in the leaves. This is where green cells called **chloroplasts** are located. Chloroplasts are the "factories" that produce glucose, a sugar.

3. The chloroplasts contain chlorophyll molecules. Chlorophyll molecules are green, and they give plants their green color. Chlorophyll traps and uses the energy found in sunlight to produce glucose.

4. The chlorophyll uses this energy from sunlight to break down water molecules (H$_2$O) into hydrogen and oxygen atoms.

5. The leaf takes carbon dioxide molecules from the air and combines them with the hydrogen atoms taken from water to produce glucose.

6. The oxygen atoms are not needed by the plant. It releases the oxygen into the atmosphere for animals to breathe. In a sense, plants are "oxygen factories" as well as sugar producers.

7. If the plant does not need all of the glucose, it is stored for future use as a **carbohydrate**, or a starch. That is what a potato is—stored starch.

More Oxygen, Please

The process of photosynthesis is important not only because it makes food for the plant and food for animals that are dependent upon plants, but also because it produces oxygen as a by-product of the process.

Look at this simple cycle and remember that when large numbers of plants are destroyed, such as a forest, oxygen is returned to the atmosphere more slowly.

The first land animals could not have existed if plants had not existed first. The Earth's early atmosphere did not contain enough oxygen for animals to exist. The first plants, probably algae, produced oxygen for the Earth's early atmosphere. Oxygen production made it possible for land animals to come into existence.

ACTION ACTIVITY
CARBON DIOXIDE AND PHOTOSYNTHESIS

One of the most important parts of the photosynthesis process requires carbon dioxide gas. Watch what happens when plants can't get CO_2.

MATERIALS
- **petroleum jelly**
- **a living plant with leaves**
- **a sunny location**

1. Find a healthy plant in a sunny location for this activity.

2. Cover one of the leaves of the plant with petroleum jelly, top and bottom. Do not remove the leaf from the plant.

3. Watch what happens to the leaf when it is unable to get carbon dioxide from the air. The leaf will begin to turn yellow as it stops making chlorophyll due to a lack of carbon dioxide.

4. See what happens if you cover leaves with petroleum jelly in the following ways:
   a. cover the top of a leaf, but not the bottom
   b. cover the bottom of a leaf, but not the top

5. Continue to compare these leaves to the normal leaves of the plant.

Leaves on many trees turn different colors in the fall, just as the leaves in this experiment changed color. When the chlorophyll production within the leaf stops due to the temperature changes and the different amounts of sunlight present in the fall, the leaves begin to change from green to other colors. Many trees and shrubs have yellow and orange pigment in their leaves, and these colors begin to show when they are no longer hidden by the chlorophyll.

Animals

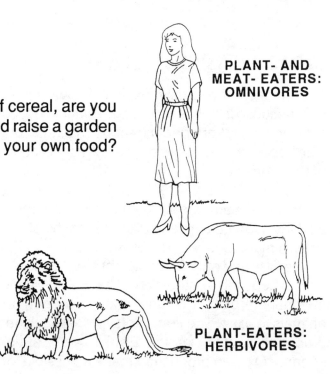

PLANT- AND MEAT- EATERS: OMNIVORES

When you fix a sandwich or prepare a bowl of cereal, are you producing your own food? If you plant seeds and raise a garden that is filled with vegetables, are you producing your own food?

The Consumers

Animals can find food, prepare food, and even raise food, but they can't produce food. We have seen that plants, with the help of chlorophyll, are the producers of all food.

Plants have to produce a lot of food because animals consume a large percentage of what plants produce. Animals can be placed in groups based upon their diets: plant-eaters, meat-eaters, and both plant- and meat-eaters.

PLANT-EATERS: HERBIVORES

MEAT-EATERS: CARNIVORES

FIND IT

Zoologists, scientists who study animals, have a basic way of classifying all animals into two groups. They do this by examining the body structure of an animal. These two groups of animals are those with backbones, called **vertebrates,** and those without backbones, called **invertebrates.** Look at the sea floor illustrated on this page and see how many vertebrates you can find. How many invertebrates can you find?

Hint: Some animals, like crabs, have external skeletons, but they do not have internal bones like a chicken or fish. Animals must have internal bone structure to be vertebrates.

ACTION ACTIVITY
SIMPLE OBSERVATION HABITATS

Look at the illustrations of simple observation habitats on this page. They are all simple to make if you look at each set of illustrations carefully. Which habitat will you make?

BUTTERFLY HABITAT
MATERIALS
- tall gift box with lid
- scissors
- clear plastic wrap
- screen mesh
- clear tape
- paper towel
- plastic flower
- modeling clay
- cotton ball
- 1 tablespoon of sugar
- 1 tablespoon of water

1. Have an adult helper cut windows in the sides and top of the gift box.
2. Tape the clear plastic wrap over the windows and the screen mesh over the top.
3. Place a paper towel in the bottom of the box.
4. Use modeling clay to form a stand for the flower. Stand the flower in the box.
5. Carefully catch a butterfly for observation, and place it in the habitat.
6. Mix the water and sugar together in a small cup or jar.
7. Soak a small piece of cotton ball in the sugar water, and place it in the middle of the flower.
8. The butterfly will rest on the flower. Watch the butterfly lap up the "flower nectar" with its long tongue when it gets hungry.
9. Do not keep the butterfly longer than 24 hours.

REPTILE/AMPHIBIAN HABITAT
MATERIALS
- 1-gallon jar with lid
- sand and small rocks
- water

1. Have an adult helper punch small holes in the lid of the 1-gallon jar to allow air into the jar when it is sealed.
2. Place a layer of sand in the jar. Add several small rocks.
3. Carefully catch a small lizard or skink, and place it in the jar for observation.
4. With your fingers, sprinkle a small amount of water into the jar for the reptile to drink. Most reptiles drink dew.
5. Do not keep the reptile longer than 48 hours.

IMPORTANT TO REMEMBER: Never keep living animals from the wild longer than two or three days. Return them to nature exactly where you originally found them. Do not take an animal out of its natural setting if you cannot return it to that setting.

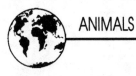

Oxygen for Animal Life

Run a race, play basketball, or swim laps for a long period of time and you will get out of breath. Your body seems to need more oxygen, and you begin to breathe harder and faster. Why?

Animals need oxygen to convert the food they eat into energy. They do this through a process called **respiration**. Respiration takes place in two stages. When oxygen is taken in, it is called **inspiration**, and when carbon dioxide gas is let out, it is called **expiration**.

A Look Inside

1. As an animal breathes in, the oxygen that is taken into the lungs moves into the blood system. It is picked up by red blood cells, and these oxygen-rich cells become bright red.

2. The blood passes through the body, carrying the blood that has oxygen in it from the lungs to the heart, where it is pumped by the heart through the animal's entire body. The animal's body is made of cells that need oxygen to digest food and produce heat and energy.

3. As the body cells use the oxygen to produce heat and energy, carbon dioxide gas is produced. The red blood cells have lost their oxygen, so they pick up the carbon dioxide gas and become very dark red.

4. The blood moves through the body and back to the heart. The blood vessels of an animal appear blue because the dark red blood looks blue through the skin.

5. The heart now pumps this carbon dioxide-filled blood to the lungs. The carbon dioxide leaves the blood and passes into the lungs, where it mixes with air.

6. The lungs force out the carbon dioxide mixture so they can take in more oxygen-rich air, and the process begins again.

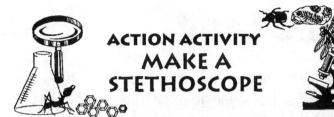

ACTION ACTIVITY
MAKE A STETHOSCOPE

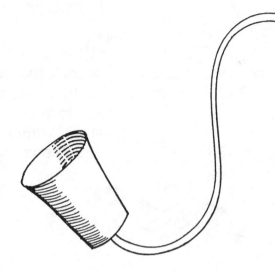

You can make a stethoscope for listening to your heart as it pumps blood throughout your body. The first stethoscope, made from a wooden tube, was developed by a French physician.

MATERIALS
- **paper or plastic cup**
- **18-inch (45.7-cm) length of plastic tubing, ¼ inch (6.25 mm) in diameter**

1. Punch a hole in the bottom of the cup with a sharpened pencil or a nail. Stick the tubing through the hole, leaving a ½ inch (12 mm) length of tubing inside the cup.

2. The tubing should be held in place by the edges of the hole, but you can make sure it stays by dabbing rubber cement around the tube at both sides of the hole.

3. After the cement has dried, put the open end of the cup over the center of your chest. Hold the loose end of the tube up to your ear. DO NOT PUT THE TUBE INTO YOUR EAR, AS YOU MIGHT DAMAGE YOUR EARDRUM. Listen closely, and you can hear your heartbeat.

ACTION ACTIVITY
BALANCED BREATHING

All body cells need oxygen to function properly. When body cells take in oxygen and give off carbon dioxide, it is called **respiration.**

MATERIALS
- **clock or watch with second hand**
- **stethoscope**
- **body thermometer**

1. The cells of our body produce heat and energy as they use oxygen and release carbon dioxide gas. Stand still and count the number of times you breathe in a minute.

2. Listen to your heartbeat through your stethoscope. Count how many times your heat beats in a minute.

3. Take your temperature. Remember what it is, or write it down.

4. Run in place for at least three minutes. Quickly count your breaths in a minute, count your heartbeat in a minute, and take your temperature.

5. What has happened? Why have the rates increased? Your body cells have to produce more energy quickly to replace the energy you use as you exercise. Your body needs lots of oxygen to produce this energy. You breathe faster, your heart pumps the blood to the cells faster, and your body produces heat as a result of the oxygen-carbon dioxide exchange.

Back to the Land

When an animal dies, it will eventually decay, or rot, and the elements that composed its body will go back into the soil. In the soil, these elements will be dissolved in water, ready for plant roots to absorb them, thus placing important elements back into the chain of life. **Decomposers** cause organisms to decay so that this process can take place.

Consumers Help Decomposers

Are buzzards and crows decomposers? No, these birds are consumers. They eat the dead animal, called **carrion,** and return it to the soil through their waste, or excrement. The buzzards do not eat all of the carrion; other, smaller organisms "eat" the rest of the dead animal. These organisms are decomposers.

What Are Decomposers?

There are two groups of decomposers: **fungi** and **bacteria**. Mold on old bread and a mushroom in the park are common examples of fungi. Bacteria (single-celled organisms that are present everywhere) are decomposers that are too small to see. They are sometimes called "germs."

As decomposers feed upon dead organisms, these organisms rot, or break down. The smell of something rotting comes from the waste or excrement of the decomposer as it digests its food and excretes it.

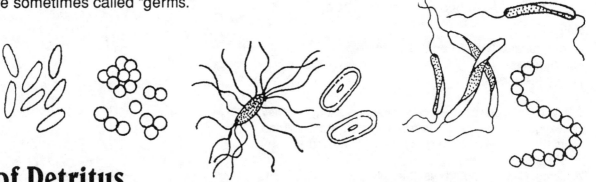

A Diet of Detritus

Dead organic matter — such as leaves, grass, wood, animal remains, and waste matter — collects on the ground to form what is called **detritus**. Decomposers break this dead matter down into smaller particles called **humus**. Humus mixes with the inorganic particles of soil, such as sediments, supplying vital nutrients for plant growth. It is a natural "fertilizer."

ACTION ACTIVITY
DETRITUS AND
HUMUS FACTORY

Decaying and decomposing matter is good for the soil. You can turn lawn clippings into detritus and humus.

MATERIALS
• **1-gallon (3.8-liter) glass jar**
• **grass clippings**
• **water**
• **soil**
• **marker**

1. Fill the bottom of the jar with 2 inches of soil.

2. Water the soil until it is wet, but not soggy.

3. Cover the top of the soil with 1 inch of grass clippings. Find these in a yard or park that has been recently mowed.

4. Draw a line on the outside of the jar at the top of the clippings.

5. Leave the container in a safe location where you can observe it for several weeks. It is best if this location is not in direct sun, but gets lots of sunlight. Do not place a lid on the container.

6. Add water every two or three days. Keep the jar warm and the grass and soil damp with water.

①

③

②

④

7. Do you see any changes in the detritus as time passes? How does it change in color? How does it change in height above the soil? Do you see any mold or fungus growing on your detritus? Look at several pieces of the grass with a magnifying glass or a microscope.

8. If you leave the detritus in the jar long enough for the decomposers to break it down, you will have a layer of humus on top of your soil. As this humus mixes with the soil below, it will eventually become topsoil, full of nutrients for plant growth.

9. You can make detritus and humus on a larger scale by making a compost pile. Find an out-of-the-way area in your backyard. Make a pile of leaves and grass clippings. Leave it alone for several weeks and watch it decay into detritus and humus. Spread it in your garden or around bushes and flower beds. It makes great "plant food."

You can also add food waste (old leftovers, spoiled food, coffee grounds, eggshells, etc.—but no meat or dairy products) to the pile, and mix in a shovelful of dirt. Every two weeks, mix up the pile with a shovel to let air get in. You can even add earthworms from a bait shop or your backyard! They love decaying matter, and help to break it down.

97

Investigating Fungi and Bacteria

Mushrooms are sold in the fruit and vegetable department of a grocery store, but they are not fruits or vegetables. In fact, they are not even plants. All mushrooms, including those on a mushroom pizza, are fungi. Order a fungi and cheese pizza sometime and see if the restaurant understands what you want!

Fungi

Mushrooms are related to yeast and mold, including the single-cell mold that is used to make penicillin. Fungi do not have chlorophyll; therefore, they cannot make their own food. Fungi get their food by secreting an enzyme that breaks down the cells of living or dead plants and animals into nutrients and absorbing them. There are nearly 90,000 species of fungi. Yeasts are some of the smallest, and giant toadstools are some of the largest.

ACTION ACTIVITY
THE GOOD, THE BAD, THE UGLY: GROWING MOLDS

It is easy to raise a miniature mold garden in a glass jar. Try it and see what your garden grows.

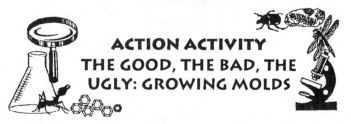

MATERIALS
- **half piece of bread**
- **small piece of cheese**
- **3 glass jars with lids**
- **orange peel or peel of any fruit**

1. Rub the half piece of bread lightly across the kitchen floor. Place the bread in a jar and sprinkle water on it. Seal the jar and place it in a warm, dark location.

2. Cut a small piece of cheese, about 1 inch long, and place it in another jar. Place the fruit peel in the last jar. Seal both jars and place them in a warm, dark location.

3. Watch for mold on all three foods. It will take different amounts of time for the mold to form on each.

4. Look at the illustration of mold and its spore cases on this page. Using a magnifying glass or microscope, watch for the development of spore cases on your gardens of mold.

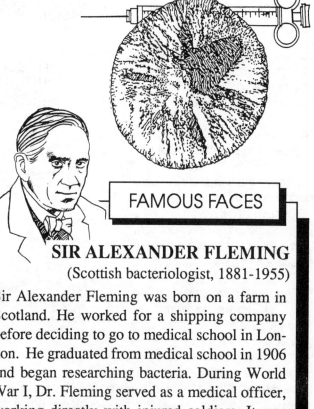

FAMOUS FACES

SIR ALEXANDER FLEMING
(Scottish bacteriologist, 1881-1955)

Sir Alexander Fleming was born on a farm in Scotland. He worked for a shipping company before deciding to go to medical school in London. He graduated from medical school in 1906 and began researching bacteria. During World War I, Dr. Fleming served as a medical officer, working directly with injured soldiers. It was during this time that he realized the need for a medicine to help cure infections. His experiments and research led to the use of a fungus called Penicillium as the first **antibiotic,** or bacteria-destroying medicine.

Bacteria

Bacteria are living organisms, the smallest form of life, but like fungi, they are neither plants nor animals. Many bacteria are very beneficial. Animals have bacteria in their digestive systems that help them break down food and nutrients. Bacteria also break down dead plants and animals into **humus** for the soil.

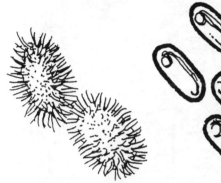

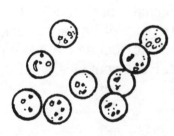

Different types of bacteria magnified thousands of times.

It is nearly impossible to touch anything without touching bacteria. Even in a sterilized environment, like a hospital operating room, it is difficult to get rid of all the bacteria. It has been estimated that if all the bacteria in the world were to be collected, they would weigh 20 times more than all other living organisms put together.

Each bacterium reproduces very quickly by dividing in half. Every 30 minutes it divides and forms new bacteria. If reproduction continued for 24 hours, this single bacterium would produce 280,000,000,000,000 (280 trillion) bacteria.

ACTION ACTIVITY
GROWING YEAST

Yeast is a one-celled organism that belongs to the fungi family. You can grow your own yeast.

MATERIALS
- **1 package of dry yeast**
- **warm water**
- **a glass or a glass jar**
- **sugar**

1. Dissolve 1 teaspoon (5 ml) of sugar in a glass of warm water.

2. Add 1 package of yeast. Place the jar in a warm location indoors.

3. Watch what happens to the contents of the jar over a period of 24 hours.

4. Do you see bubbles in the yeast mixture? The yeast produced carbon dioxide gas. This gas is what makes yeast bread "rise," or fill the pan, before it is baked. If you look closely at bread, you will see small air pockets in the bread caused by the gas.

5. Leave the yeast mixture alone for several days. Smell the mixture. You are smelling ethyl alcohol. Yeast causes the sugar water to ferment, and ethyl alcohol and carbon dioxide gas are produced.

Regions of Life on Earth

If you were given one million dollars and told you could go to any place you wanted to go, for any amount of time, where would you go? What would you do? Humans can go anywhere they want to go, if they have the time and the money. The world is truly getting smaller as transportation becomes faster and more widely available.

Giant Habitat

There is a very important reason why people can travel to any spot on Earth: the entire Earth is a giant habitat for humans. People live just about everywhere. There are people living in the frigid polar regions and the arid deserts, but the largest population groupings are found in **temperate zones**, or areas that do not suffer from extreme temperature changes. These are areas where people do not have to **adapt**, or change, their lives drastically because of the environment.

Plants and animals are much more limited. They cannot wear coats to keep warm or buy food at a store when they are hungry. They live in smaller habitats that provide the food and nutrients needed and a temperature range that they can live in easily. Plants and animals can adapt to changes in the environment, but it takes

time — sometimes millions of years.

Different types of animals are found in the different environmental regions of the Earth. Look at the environmental regions illustrated here and on the following pages. How would life differ in each environment?

Rain Forest: Just as there are many levels to a high-rise building, there are also many levels of plant and animal life in a rain forest. The conditions for life on each level can be very different from conditions on the other levels. The two main regions of life in a rain forest are the **canopy,** or the treetops, and the **ground.** In this warm, dark, wet environment, decay takes place quickly, returning nutrients to the soil which in turn are used by the rapidly growing plants. Some plants and animals are brightly colored, and others, like the sloth, which has algae in its fur, blend into this world of green.

Polar Regions: Because of the severe cold, there are fewer species of plants, animals, and decomposers in the polar regions than in any other region of the world. Plants such as lichens, mosses, grasses, and shrubs grow close to the ground for warmth and protection from strong winds. Because temperatures stay below freezing most of the year, decomposition takes place very slowly and it takes a long time for nutrients to be replaced in the soil. Most of the animals in this region have small ears and tails so they do not lose their much-needed body heat. Thick fur or thick layers of body fat also help these animals to retain body heat. Fur can even be found on the foot pads of many arctic animals, protecting their feet from the ice and snow while giving them added traction on the frozen land.

Deserts: Desert life is affected by low rainfall, high evaporation, and drastic temperature changes between day and night. When rain does fall, it is often heavy, and most of it runs off the surface quickly, taking nutrients and soil with it to basins and gullies. Desert plants and animals have adapted to the small amount of water available in arid, dry regions. Cacti have thin, sharp-pointed needles instead of flat, broad leaves. This prevents them from losing moisture through their leaves. Many desert animals excrete dry urine pellets (pack rat) or very dry feces (jack rabbit) to retain as much body moisture as possible. The lack of water and the scalding heat of the Sun force many desert animals to find shade or an underground burrow during the hottest hours of the day, venturing out at night and during the early morning hours when it is cooler.

Grasslands: Grasslands are usually gently rolling to flat lands that get too much rain to be called a desert, but not enough rain to sustain trees. Water evaporates quickly in these regions, and severe droughts are common. Most grassland animals graze or burrow. They usually live in family groups, herds, or packs to help each other. This togetherness allows some of the animals to graze while others look out for danger, and it allows their predators to hunt and bring down animals larger than themselves. Many of the animals grazing on grasslands have long legs and are good runners. Their long legs help them to run through the tall grass and low shrubs that cover the land. The animals depend upon speed to get away from their enemies, which are also fast runners.

Aquatic Regions: There are three aquatic regions of life on Earth—fresh water; salt water; and brackish water, where fresh water and salt water come together. All plants and animals that live in water have to be able to obtain gases from the water. Animals have developed gills and other means for obtaining oxygen and other gases from the water. Water plants remove CO_2 from the water and produce O_2 as a by-product of photosynthesis. Since water plants need light for photosynthesis, they are found only in water that is shallow enough for sunlight to filter through. Because of this, the majority of all aquatic plants are found within the first few feet of the water's surface. Even the smallest freshwater algae and saltwater plant plankton need sunlight. Unlike plants, animals are able to adapt to life in all regions of water. There are surface dwellers, bottom dwellers, and those that are free swimmers, or able to move throughout the different regions. Most water animals are found where there is an abundance of plant life available for food, but many water animals live in deeper areas and prey upon other water animals.

Mountains: Because mountains are so high in elevation, they provide several different levels, or regions, for plant and animal life. The lower regions are warmer and covered with many different kinds of trees and shrubs. Both large and small animals, such as deer, fox, squirrels, birds, and mice, are found there. The higher the mountain level, the colder the temperatures, the thinner the air, and the more rocky the terrain. Plants become smaller and there are fewer animals. On very tall mountains there is a line where the larger trees stop growing and only smaller plants grow. This is called the **timberline**. Animals have to be agile and strong to be able to move about on the steep, rocky land above the timberline. Mountain goats are expert climbers and are often seen on even the higher levels of mountains.

Forests: Many different kinds of plants and animals are found living in the different levels of a forest—on the ground, under the ground, and in the trees. These levels of life are affected by the level of light available to them. The top of the forest receives the most light, and the trees grow thick and tall as they compete for light. Less sunlight is able to penetrate through to the lower levels of the trees, making it difficult for low-growing plants to survive. Most animal life is found on or under the forest floor. Forest animals are difficult to see because they tend to be the same colors as the forest. Deer, squirrels, fox, raccoons, and birds blend into their surroundings. This blending is called **camouflage**. Many forest animals live alone except when mating and raising their young. These animals can live within a small area because food and water are usually easy to find. Organic matter, such as leaves and feces, rots and decays quickly on the damp forest floor, providing nutrients for the plants and for the animals that eat the plants.

Chapter 7

Our Changing Earth

Because you were born, the Earth will be changed. Your cat or dog, the plants in your house, and the grass around your school change the Earth in some small ways. Even an insect hatched from an egg deep in a rain forest will cause the Earth to be different. The lithosphere, hydrosphere, and atmosphere are all important to life, and in turn, life uses the resources provided by these parts of the Earth.

As soon as life formed on Earth, the Earth began to change. Blue-green algae produced oxygen that filtered into the water and the atmosphere. As more and more oxygen formed and ozone developed in the atmosphere, the plants and animals began the cycle of life, the cycle of food, the cycle of carbon, the cycle of nitrogen, and on and on.

It is impossible for the Earth to stay the same because each living organism changes it in many ways. Let's look at the past and present changes the Earth has undergone and continues to undergo because of life.

Changes

Humans can adapt to their surroundings, but because of their intelligence, they are also able to change their environment. Mankind learned early that it was easier to modify the environment to make life more comfortable than to wait for the natural processes of environmental change, which occur slowly. Humans are able to make changes more quickly.

Early Americans

The early Native Americans believed in caring for their environment. They respected nature because it was their provider. They hunted animals for food and fur, gathered plants for food and dye, used plant and animal products to make their shelter, used clay from the earth for pots, and chiseled stones for weapons.

Archaeologists know about the early Native Americans because of the way in which they cared for and changed the world around them. They have found campsites 500 years old where rocks had been moved, fires had been built, wood had been gathered and burned, and small pieces of chipped flint remain to tell the story of arrowhead production.

The Earth was changed by these people, but so slightly that it is difficult today to find evidence of their existence.

A Look at Modern Life

Archaeologists in the future who might dig up a modern "campsite" — a house — would see hundreds of ways in which the world was changed by the people who inhabited the house.

Today, people are changing the Earth at such an alarming rate that it is difficult to understand how all of the changes will affect our environment — present and future. Because of the many advances made in technology over the past 200 years, evidence of modern human existence will last for many, many years to come. That's why we have to be very careful to take care of our environment.

Caring for the Earth's Land

We live in a "throwaway" society. Over the past 40 years, modern technology has created products that are designed to be used and then thrown away. The packaging that "sells" the products has become big and attention-getting, sometimes even more important and expensive than the product itself. We buy these products and then discard all of the unneeded packaging. Where does all of this trash go? The last time we see it is in garbage cans or in the garbage truck that picks it up. When it is gone, we tend to forget about it.

Where Does the Trash Go?

Everything we throw away has to go somewhere, and much of it goes into landfills. What happens when trash is placed in landfills? As the garbage rots and decays, it builds up heat and gases, mostly methane. These gases escape from the rotting trash and pollute the atmosphere. As the inside of this big pile continues to "cook," chemicals, dyes, and inks used on the materials that have become trash mix with others and drain down to the bottom. Rain helps to carry these chemicals down through the landfill, into the soil, and finally into the ground water.

Some of our garbage is **biodegradable.** That means it is capable of decaying or rotting down into detritus or humus (p. 96), especially when exposed to sunlight and weather. Paper, food, metal cans, and lawn clippings are examples of biodegradable matter found in garbage.

Other types of trash are non-biodegradable, especially plastic. Milk and juice containers, soda bottles, toys, product packaging and wrapping, and grocery and shopping bags are a few examples of plastic items in our trash that will be around for a long, long time after they are thrown away. This is why recycling, not discarding, is so important. It keeps these non-biodegradable products out of landfills and garbage dumps, saves money and energy, and reduces pollution by factories because we don't have to produce new plastic items to replace the discarded ones.

This is just one example of how our actions affect our Earth — land, air, and water. There are very few people on Earth who do not generate trash just by meeting the needs of life. If generating trash is part of our present life, what is the solution? The first step is to become **aware** of the consequences of your actions. For example, find out what happens to your garbage. Is there a way to cut the amount of trash you discard each day? How?

We need to "think before we throw." You can help care for the Earth's land by remembering the three "R's":

REDUCE: Buy items with less packaging (especially plastic) so less trash is created.

RE-USE: Instead of throwing away plastic shopping bags, use them again to hold and store things. Cardboard and plastic boxes can also be re-used. See how many things you can re-use that you would normally throw away.

RECYCLE: Collect glass and plastic bottles and containers, newspapers, aluminum and other metal cans, and take them to a recycling center. There may even be a recycling pick-up service where you live. Look in the yellow pages of your phone book to find one. Buy products made of recycled materials or packaged with recycled materials.

Caring for the Earth's Water

Water. You turn on your faucet at home and there it is, as much as you want, whenever you need it. Water seems to be abundant, but it isn't. Only 1% of all of the Earth's water is fresh water that we can drink and use. It is a very precious and limited resource. We need this water to live. If it gets polluted, what will we drink?

Water Pollution

We have learned that most of our fresh water is underground (p. 66). Anything we put on or in the ground can eventually move down through the soil and into the ground water. Pesticides, fertilizers, factory waste, chemicals, and oil are just a few of the things people "get rid of" by dumping on the ground or burying in dumps. One quart of used motor oil can pollute as much as a million gallons of ground water! People used to think that by burying or dumping waste it would somehow disappear. It is like looking at something you do not like and closing your eyes—you do not see it anymore, but it is still there. We are now beginning to realize that the "dump it and forget it" attitude is harmful to the environment, especially our ground water—the very water we drink.

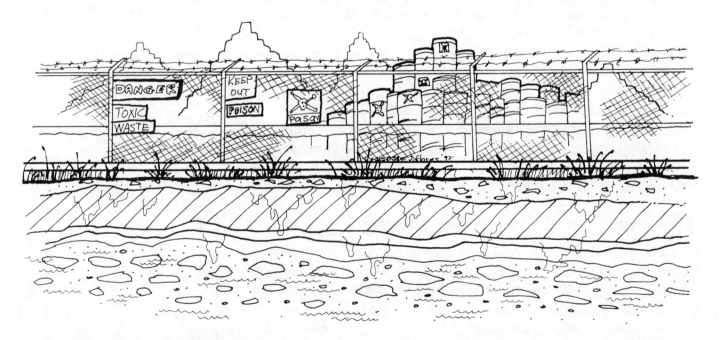

Fresh Water Waste

In the United States alone, we use 450,000,000,000 (450 billion) gallons of water **every day**. How do we use so much water? Just think about it: brushing teeth, washing hands, taking a shower or bath, watering the houseplants and yard, washing the car, washing the dishes, washing clothes. We can't stop using water in our daily lives, but we can make sure that we don't use more than we really need. The first step is to become **aware** of how much water we use during the day and then decide how much of this is needed and how much is wasteful. We can help today by reducing our water use.

Caring for the Earth's Atmosphere

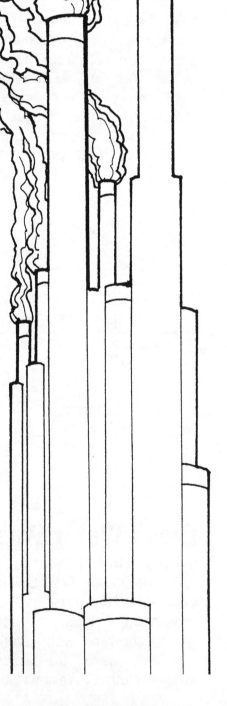

Look around your house. Almost everything runs on electricity: the TV, stereo, radio, stove, refrigerator, dishwasher, clothes washer and dryer, all of the lights, the air conditioner, and maybe even the heater. Think about your friends' homes. They probably use electricity, too. How many homes are using electricity in this country? in the world? Where does all of this electricity come from?

Air Pollution

Electrical generating plants, or "power plants," supply most of our electricity. One way to generate electricity is to burn something to create heat. A lot of power plants burn coal and oil. When these fossil fuels are burned, they release chemicals — sulfur dioxides and nitrogen oxides — into the atmosphere. These chemicals mix with the gases and water vapor in the atmosphere to form sulfuric acid. This acid collects in rain clouds and falls to earth mixed with rain, snow, sleet, and hail. When this happens it is called "acid rain."

Acid rain affects plants, animals, and people. It can harm trees, poison lakes and rivers, and kill fish. As an acid, it even damages some buildings and statues. (See page 50.) Acid rain is becoming a big problem as we continue to fill the atmosphere with polutants.

Things You Can Do Today to Help

You can make sure you and your family do not waste electricity. Remember, the more electricity we use, the more the power plants burn coal and oil. Exhaust from cars also contributes to air pollution and acid rain. Here are some things you can do to help:

1. Bike, skateboard, roller-skate, or walk instead of riding in a car whenever you can.
2. Turn off lights when they are not needed. Don't leave televisions and radios on when no one is watching or listening.
3. Use a microwave oven or toaster oven instead of the stove. Microwave ovens use only $\frac{1}{3}$ to $\frac{1}{2}$ as much energy as a stove.
4. Whenever possible, use ceiling fans or portable fans instead of air conditioning. Check for "air leaks" at doors and windows.
5. Keep the refrigerator and freezer doors closed. Don't leave them open longer than it takes to reach in and out.

You Can Help

Now that you know so much about the Earth, you will be able to make decisions about how you live your life based upon your knowledge of how the Earth works. It is important to know the consequences of your actions. For more information on how you can help by being environmentally wise, contact the following organizations:

Alliance to Save Energy
1725 K Street NW, Ste 914
Washington, DC 20006

Center for Marine Conservation
1725 DeSales Street NW, Ste 500
Washington, DC 20036

The Children's Rainforest
P.O. Box 936
Lewiston, ME 04240

Coastal Conservation Association
P.O. Box 1630
Fulton, TX 78358

Cousteau Society
930 W. 21st Street
Norfolk, VA 23517

Creating Our Future
398 North Ferndale
Mill Valley, CA 94941

Defenders of Wildlife
1244 19th Street NW
Washington, DC 20036

The Earth-based Magazine for Kids
P.O. Box 52
Montgomery, VT 05470

Earth Communications Office
P.O. Box 36M39, #207
Los Angeles, CA 90036

The Environmental Defense Fund
1616 P Street NW, Suite 150
Washington, DC 20036

Greenpeace
1436 U Street NW
Washington, DC 20009

Izaak Walton League of America
1401 W. Blvd., Level B
Arlington, VA 22209

Kids Against Pollution
P.O. Box 775 High Street
Closter, NJ 07624

The Kid's Earth Works Group
1400 Shattuck Avenue, #25
Berkeley, CA 94709

National Audubon Society
950 Third Avenue
New York, NY 10022

National Wildlife Federation
1400 16th Street NW
Washington, DC 20036

The National Resources Defense Council
40 West 20th Street
New York, NY 10011

Nature Conservancy
1815 N. Lynn Street
Arlington, VA 22209

Sierra Club
730 Polk Street
San Francisco, CA 94109

Take Pride in America
P.O. Box 1339-Y
Jessup, MD 20794

Trees for Life
1103 Jefferson
Wichita, KS 67203

U.S. Department of Agriculture
P.O. Box 96090
Washington, DC 20250

U.S. Department of Energy
P.O. Box 8900
Silver Spring, MD 20907

U.S. Environmental Protection Agency
401 M Street SW, PM 211B
Washington, DC 20460

Whale Center
3933 Piedmont Ave, Ste #2
Oakland, CA 94611

World Wildlife Fund
1250 24th Street NW
Washington, DC 20037

Glossary

A

air pressure The pressing of all of the air in the atmosphere against everything it touches on the Earth's surface. Air pressure is greatest next to the surface; the higher you go in the atmosphere, the less air pressure there is.

atmosphere The layer of gases that surrounds the Earth, forming a protective shield from the Sun's harmful radiation.

atom The smallest complete particle of matter. Atoms are the building blocks that make up all matter. Each atom is made up of three smaller parts: protons, neutrons, electrons.

axis An imaginary line running through the center of the Earth from the North Pole to the South Pole. The line is tilted 23.5 degrees, and this tilting is responsible for the Earth's seasons.

C

cloud A large group of tiny water droplets that join together in the atmosphere.

compound A molecule that combines at least two different types of atoms.

condensation The changing of a gas, or vapor, into a liquid. Condensation takes place above the Earth when warm, moist air (vapor) rises into the cooler regions of the atmosphere and the rising air changes into liquid water, or precipitation, such as rain, snow, sleet, or hail.

constructive boundary The area or crack in the Earth's surface between plates (giant pieces of the lithosphere). These cracks occur due to the very gradual movement of the plates within the surface.   Also called a construction zone, this area allows magma from the asthenosphere to work its way to the surface, forming—or constructing—new crust.

convection The movement of air heated by the Sun. This movement causes hot air to rise from the surface into the atmosphere, where it cools and falls back to the surface. The air is re-heated and rises again, creating a great circle or current called a convection cell.

core The center of the Earth. The inner core, at the very center, is solid. The outer core, just outside the inner core, is molten iron and nickel.

crust The thin, solid outer layer of the Earth. The thick layer of rock that forms the continents is called the sial layer. It is made of granite. The thin layer under the continents, called the sima layer, also forms the ocean floor. The sima layer is made of basalt.

D

destructive boundary The area of the Earth's surface where the crust, or lithosphere, is destroyed. These areas are created when plates collide, pushing one plate under the crust of the other. The "disappearing" plate then is melted, or "destroyed," in the mantle. Also called a subduction zone.

E

Earth The only planet in our Solar System with the right environment for life to exist. It is a solid planet, and nearly $\frac{3}{4}$ of its surface is covered with water. Earth is the only planet with liquid water.

earthquake The sudden movement of the Earth's crust caused by the release of pressure from deep within the Earth. In a severe earthquake, giant cracks may appear in the Earth's surface.

element A combination of at least two atoms of the same type. Scientists have discovered 109 elements. They are grouped into a list called the periodic table according to their atomic number, or the number of electrons in one atom of the element. The six most common elements are oxygen, silicon, aluminum, iron, calcium, and sodium.

erosion The removal of broken pieces of rock by changes to the Earth's surface, such as rain, ice, acid, and wind.

Equator An imaginary circle around the middle of the Earth, which divides the Earth into the Northern Hemisphere and the Southern Hemisphere.

evaporation The changing of a liquid into a vapor. Evaporation occurs when the Sun heats water, and the liquid water molecules change to gas and rise through the air, mixing with other gases.

G

gas The lightest elements. The gases oxygen and nitrogen make up our atmosphere, which forms a protective layer around the Earth and shields us from the Sun's harmful radiation.

geographic pole An imaginary point through which the Earth's axis of rotation passes.

glacier A thick, dense layer of ice formed by layers of snow that built up over a period of many years. Glaciers form in the valleys and snowfields between mountain peaks.

gravity The force with which the Earth pulls everything on its surface and in the sky toward its center. Gravity pulls at objects in space, too, but its force decreases the further you move away from the center of the Earth.

H

humidity Moisture, or water vapor, in the air. The relative humidity is a measure of the moisture compared to the maximum amount the air could hold at the present temperature.

hydrosphere The liquid surface of the Earth; the ocean.

I

igneous The type of rock formed when magma (very hot liquid rock in the middle of the Earth) works its way into the crust and then cools and hardens.

L

lava Very hot liquid rock from the Earth's mantle that breaks through the surface of the crust. When lava is found in the mantle, it is called magma.

liquid A state of matter that flows and takes the shape of its container.

lithosphere The solid surface of the Earth; the crust.

M

magnetic pole An imaginary point through which the Earth's magnetic axis passes. It is tilted 11 degrees away from the axis of rotation.

mantle The middle section of the Earth, made of thick, solid rock.

matter The substance of which all objects on Earth are made. Anything that takes up space and has weight is matter. It is usually divided into three groups — solids, liquids, and gases.

metamorphic Igneous or sedimentary rock that has been changed into a different kind of rock by extreme heat and pressure. Metamorphic rock is formed below the surface of the crust.

minerals The different combinations of elements that make up the rocks that form the Earth's crust.

molecule A combination of two or more atoms. Everything on Earth is made of either molecules of the pure elements, or molecules with combinations of elements, called compounds.

mountain Land that extends at least 2,000 feet above sea level. A true mountain will have at least two different areas, or zones, of climate and life. Mountains cover about one fifth of the Earth's surface.

O

oceanography The study of the geography of the ocean floor.

ozone A combination of free oxygen (single atoms of oxygen) and oxygen molecules (O_2) that forms a layer above the Earth. This ozone layer absorbs most of the Sun's harmful ultraviolet radiation.

P

phase A stage in the appearance of the Moon during the month it takes the Moon to make one complete circle around the Earth. The phases change gradually as the amount of light that the Moon reflects from the Sun changes.

photosynthesis The process simple plants use to produce their own food, using carbon dioxide, water, and sunlight.

planet A ball-shaped body in space that moves in an oval-shaped path around a star. The nine planets in our Solar System are Mercury, Venus, Earth, Mars, Jupiter, Saturn, Uranus, Neptune, and Pluto.

plate tectonics The very slow movement of the continents as they drift apart from each other. This slow drifting movement, too slow to be felt, is due to the movement of the partially molten layer of Earth under the continents—the asthenosphere. Also called continental drift.

precipitation Liquid water that forms in the clouds and falls to Earth in the form of rain, snow, sleet, or hail.

R

revolution The path or orbit a planet makes as it circles the Sun.

rotation The spinning movement the Earth makes on its axis. One complete rotation equals 23 hours and 56 minutes.

S

Solar System The Sun and the nine planets (including Earth) and their moons which move in an elliptical (oval-shaped) path around the Sun.

solid Any substance with shape and volume that is not a liquid or a gas. One of the three states of matter.

Sun The huge, fiery-hot star at the center of our Solar System. The Sun gives off light and heat energy. Without the Sun, life on Earth could not exist.

sedimentary The type of rock formed by layers of sediments, loose materials deposited together by water, wind, or glacier ice.

T

trench A deep valley in the ocean floor. Trenches are created in destructive boundaries, or subduction zones, where movement of plates in the Earth's crust forces one plate underneath another and destroys part of the crust. The deepest trench is the Mariana Trench, approximately 36,400 feet deep in the Pacific Ocean.

tsunami A giant ocean wave caused by an earthquake under the ocean floor. A tsunami often moves across the ocean into land, causing damage and death.

U

ultraviolet radiation The Sun's invisible, harmful rays. Many of these rays are filtered out by the Earth's atmosphere.

V

volcano An opening in the Earth's crust that releases gases and molten rock, or lava, which have been building up pressure in a chamber beneath the crust. Volcanoes are formed over very hot spots in the Earth's mantle, and they explode where there is a weak spot in the crust.

W

weather The results of the Sun's effect on the Earth's solid and water surfaces, such as temperature, rainfall, wind speed, and humidity.

weathering The process that occurs when rocks are constantly broken into smaller pieces. Two kinds of weathering wear down the surface of the Earth: physical and chemical changes.

Index

HAVE MORE FUN WITH SCIENCE...
JOIN THE SCIENCE FOR EVERY KID CLUB!

Just fill in the coupon below and mail to:
FAN CLUB HEADQUARTERS/F. Nachbaur
John Wiley & Sons, 605 Third Avenue, New York, NY 10158

Name_____

Address_____

City_____ State_____ ZIP_____

Membership in the Science for Every Kid Club entitles you to a quarterly news-letter featuring science tidbits, games, and other experiments, plus other surprises...and it's free!!!

✂ --

Exciting and Fun Science Activity Books
from Everyone's Favorite Science Teacher...Janice VanCleave

Mail to: John Wiley & Sons, Inc. 605 Third Avenue
New York, NY 10158 Attn: F. Nachbaur

To order by Phone:

☎

**Call Toll-Free
1-800-US-WILEY**

___ ANIMALS (55052-3), @ $9.95
___ EARTHQUAKES (57107-5), @ $9.95
___ GRAVITY (55050-7), @ $9.95
___ MACHINES (57108-3), @ $9.95
___ MAGNETS (57106-7), @ $9.95
___ MOLECULES (55054-X), @ $9.95
___ ASTRONOMY FOR EVERY KID (53573-7), @ $10.95
___ BIOLOGY FOR EVERY KID (50381-9), @ $10.95
___ CHEMISTRY FOR EVERY KID (62085-8), @ $10.95
___ EARTH SCIENCE FOR EVERY KID (53010-7), @ $10.95
___ MATH FOR EVERY KID (54265-2), @ $10.95
___ PHYSICS FOR EVERY KID (52505-7), @ $10.95
___ 200 GOOEY, SLIPPERY, SLIMY, WEIRD, AND
     FUN EXPERIMENTS (57921-1), @ $10.95

❑ Payment enclosed (Wiley pays postage & handling)
❑ Charge my __ Visa __ Mastercard __ Amex
Card #_____ Exp. Date ___/___

Name_____

Address_____

City_____ State_____ ZIP_____